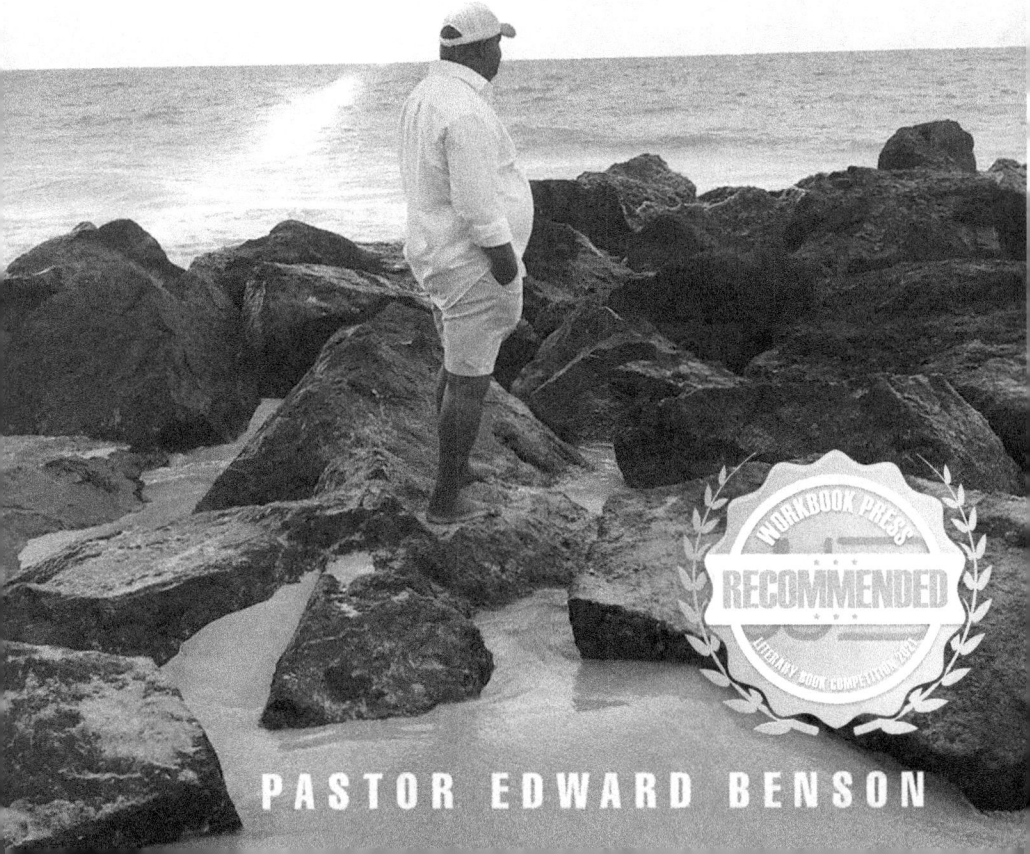

2022 CHASING THE VISION

PASTOR EDWARD BENSON

Copyright @2022 by Pastor Edward Benson

All rights reserved. No part of this book may be reproduced in any form or by any electronic or mechanical means, including information storage and retrieval systems, without permission in writing from the publisher, except by reviewers, who may quote brief passages in a review.

This publication contains the opinions and ideas of its author. It is intended to provide helpful and informative material on the subjects addressed in the publication. The author and publisher specifically disclaim all responsibility for any liability, loss or risk, personal or otherwise, which is incurred as a consequence, directly or indirectly, of the use and application of any of the contents of this book.

WORKBOOK PRESS LLC
187 E Warm Springs Rd,
Suite B285, Las Vegas, NV 89119, USA

Website:https://workbookpress.com/
Hotline:1-888-818-4856
Email:admin@workbookpress.com

Ordering Information:
Quantity sales. Special discounts are available on quantity purchases by corporations, associations, and others.
For details, contact the publisher at the address above.

ISBN-13:	978-1-957618-08-1 (Paperback Version)
	978-1-957618-09-8 (Digital Version)

REV. DATE:01/20/2022

2022
"CHASING THE VISION"
God Family Business

BY

PASTOR EDWARD BENSON

"I press toward the mark for the prize of the high calling of God in Christ Jesus" (Phil. 3:14). So, press on "Vision Chaser", press on.

CONTENTS

DEDICATION	i
ACKNOWLEDGEMENTS	i
INTRODUCTION	iii
WRITE THE VISION	1
CHASING THE VISION	8
WHO ARE YOU	12
YOU ARE A VISION CHASER	22
WAIT, REST & CHASE	31
VENOM & VISION	40
THE INSIDE MAN	48
PROBLEMS, PROBLEMS, PROBLEMS	57
SILENCING THE NOISE	61
GOING THE EXTRA MILE	67
GROWING UP IN CHRIST	74
VISION SHINES BRIGHT	84
REFLECTIONS	90
VISION CHASERS ARE CRAZY	98
KEEP CHASING THE VISION	106
DIRTY WORK	114
CHASE YOUR VISION-NOT SOMEBODY ELSE	124
GOD HAS A PLAN	130
HAVEN'T SEEN MY BEST YET	138

DEDICATION

I dedicate this book to Jesus Christ—my Lord, my God, my Savior, and Friend. I am grateful and honored to be called a Vision Chaser.

To my wife, Aisha Benson who always inspires me to look into the mirror and keep chasing the Vision that God has given us. We have weathered some fierce storms and by the grace and mercy of God—survived to stay in the race.

To my family at Living In Jesus Ministry, Inc. may the Word of God forever be lived, taught, and preached in Newburgh, NY and beyond.

ACKNOWLEDGMENTS

I am greatly indebted to the numerous prayer warriors who sincerely prayed for me and my family during the past twelve (12) years we have been on the battlefield as Vision Chasers.

To all who have also been called into Ministry to plant churches, start outreach ministries, start a new business, or expand an existing one, those who are casting visions for themselves and for their families—keep chasing the vision.

I could never adequately write these acknowledgments without expressing thanks to family. Wife, Aisha Benson, and children: Akeem, Malik, Adrienne, Christen, Tiffany and Alexander. Also, my grandchildren: Madison, Ariah, and future grand yet to arrive. It is my hope each of you will always be in relentless pursuit of the Vision God has given you. Always chase your dreams and be resolved that quitting is never an option! If you get a chance to sit it out or dance. I hope you all dance. **Remember: Every morning you have two choices: Keep sleeping with your dreams and visions or wake up and chase them.**

INTRODUCTION

Has God given you a vision? Has he showed you in advance an accomplishment worthy of pursuit? Has he called you to preach, teach, plant a church, open a business, run for public office, start a ministry within a church, desire more financial freedom for your family and community? If so, you already know that unless you chase the vision, it will die. Also, the more you chase the vision, the more the enemy chases after you.

If you have a vision to improve your health. Improve your finances, family relationships, your business, your mental stability, your faith, then this book needs to be read and digested. When I say vision, I'm not talking about eyesight, but those who have been given sight to originate, invent, create, build, or ignite a new and/or greater thing than currently exists for a changing world. We live in a world where people chase after fame, fortune, money, and material possessions. Yet in the midst of all of this, God is offering something more eternal: the vision to offer the plan of Salvation through Jesus Christ and the vision to create, build and change things that glorify God. This book is a must read, because it will help convict you that you must make what you are chasing a priority, and part of the chase is adopting a readiness and an endurance mindset. You must be willing to pick up your cross and chase the vision of furthering the Kingdom-work in ministry, family, and business for eternal value. You must never, never, ever quit.

Instead of us setting the pattern for the world, the world has set the pattern for us. This pandemic has changed our sense of reality and we need a written vision to put us back on course. Given these facts, Vision Chasers need reliable tips and strategies to stay on course. For example, you need to know how to:

- Write the Vision (Business Plan, Mission Statement, Flight Plan, Budget)

- Rest Up for the Chase (Take a Sabbath)

- Know your lane: Visionary, Ambassador or Future Torch Bearer

- Go the Extra Mile (Because nobody is going to do it like you do it)

- Do the Dirty Work (Evangelize/Marketing/Budgeting)

- Silence the Noise (Let the Vision be the loudest voice)

- Stay for the long haul (Don't Quit)

- Be a little crazy (Even if the store sell 25 different Candles— let yours be #26)

- Equip yourself (Study and Be Prepared for your Blessing)

- Deal with the Inside Man & Problems (Habits/ Vices/Sins)

- Be your Best and Encourage Yourself

The Covid-19 pandemic has triggered huge change in the way we worship, in consumer behavior and how we prepare for the current and future needs of our families. Online shopping and worshipping have become King, as stores and churches close around the country. In many cases families have not seen each other, except via FaceTime, Zoom or other forms of social media. Whenever we emerge from this post pandemic era the landscape will be different and look different from what we left behind. Thus, the way we view and approach our lives in the areas of ministry, business and family has to change. Our vision strategy has to evolve. **Our world needs more Vision Chasers**. Covid-19 pandemic continues to test the leadership and vision of Christians and Christian Business owners around the globe. Nevertheless, your Vision must go forth. This world needs your Vision, your dream, your success story. Whatever is at the root of your Vision or Dream, it must be the reason that drives you daily because this is marathon not a sprint that last a lifetime. If your vision is to operate a business –then your spiritual life must be fully integrated with the life of your business. If your vision is in ministry, you must chase after the rapture; the time when Jesus returns. If the vision is for your family, then God must be first in the budget and the head of the household.

Vision Chasers in ministry and business are needed today more than ever before. Because of the pandemic, we have so many churches and businesses that have closed because we have failed to pivot and build new visions to become more effective leaders in an unstable marketplace. So, in a world that keeps changing the question is: Where are the Vision Chasers? Vision Chasers – the ones called to build, ignite, energize, breathe something new or better into kingdom building and church. **Psalm 71:18** says: "and even when I am old and grey oh God do not forsake me—until I declare your strength to this generation your power to all who are to come." With every fiber in my being, I believe this is our job as Vision Chasers. Regardless of the specific direction God takes you, it is your job to love God's people. Vision Chasers, regardless of your calling, gifts, or vocation, you must chase after the rapture. Regardless of social distancing we must Sell out to the idea that our job is to spread the gospel of Jesus Christ to the world until Jesus returns. Our job is to reach our generation and the next one. We must become relentless in our pursuit because there is too much at stake.

We are all called to chase the vision. The question is where do you fit-- in the pursuit? Are you a Visionary, Ambassador, or a Future Torch Bearer? In some cases, God might anoint you to be all three.

VISIONARIES

Visionaries are people with a strong vision of the future who leads a team of Ambassadors and Torch Bearers using a practical and strategic plan to pursue goals and implement the vision. Visionaries are the people that God has given the vision directly to write down and pursue. Visionaries change the world. They are responsible for recruiting and training Ambassadors and Future Torch Bearers of the vision.

AMBASSADORS

Ambassadors are those who run with the vision alongside the Visionary to do the work and recruit others to help spread the vision. Ambassadors are the Visionaries' official representatives who represent and communicate the desires and will of the visionary to others. **2 Corinthians 5:20. The vision of Christ is that all might be saved.** As a Christian, you are an Ambassador for Christ. That is one who represents Christ.

TORCH BEARER

A Future Torch Bearer is someone who is being trained and groomed to become the next visionary by performing the day-to-day task of vision. He or she is being trained so that the current visionary can eventually pass the baton. The Future Torch Bearer stands next to the Visionary and is recognized as the next leader in a movement. They are the successor, heir and beneficiary of the Vision who will continue to impart knowledge, truth, and inspiration to others.

Every successful growing organization, business and family utilizes Visionaries, Ambassadors, and Torch Bearers. Most Christian churches are not growing during this season because they are not following God's plan for evangelizing and growth for the kingdom. The Church provide training for the title and position a person holds, but not for the calling on their life. We have deacon training, trustee training, training for ministry leaders, musicians, and choirs, but no one is being trained to be a Visionary, an Ambassador, or Future Torch Bearer. Training is paramount because **the moment you stop training people to be leaders you begin to die.** Everyone should be working together as a team and carry the same message. Democrats, Republicans, Isis, Taliban, religious cults, corporations, small businesses, Muslims, Jehovah Witnesses, and Mormons are successful when it comes to growth because everyone is taught to practice and preach the same message. Vision Chasers we must have the same message (vision) as we go forth to witness to others. Some Churches go without a Pastor for years because the previous Pastor did not have a Torch Bearer in place. There was no training or preparation for his or her successor. A part of your vision should be finding your replacement. **However, we must first have a vision worth passing on.**

WRITE THE VISION

Every morning you have two choices: Keep sleeping with your dreams and visions or wake up and chase them. If you are to be successful, your vision, business plan, and family budget and goals must be in writing. Your vision can't be fully understood or implemented without being in writing. A Vision not written will soon be forgotten. That's why God said write the vision and make it plain. In the Seventh Century BC, when the Assyrian Empire controlled Israel, the prophet Habakkuk, cried out in the fear that God had abandoned the nation forever. So, he demanded of God an answer in **Habakkuk 2:1-3.** "**Habakkuk 2:1-3** "I will stand at my watch and station myself on the ramparts; I will look to see what he will say to me, and what answer I am to give to this complaint. Then the Lord replied: *"And the Lord answered me, and said, Write the vision, and make it plain upon tables, that he may run that readeth it."* **For the revelation (vision) awaits an appointed time, it speaks of the end and will not prove false.** Though it lingers, ***wait for it:*** it will certainly come and will not delay". **Write it down** and relentlessly Chase after it.

Writing a vision seems about as helpful as shouting into a hurricane unless we believe what we write. If we take the time to articulate our hopes, dreams, our business plan, financial goals, etc. and share it as a written vision, it becomes the beginning of a shared reality. For the Vision is what we intend to grow toward.

The challenge for most vision chasers is that their leading

comes from within where others don't reside. Corralling others to carry out the vision becomes difficult when you don't have a playbook for them to follow. In Ministry you need a written Vision. In Business you need a Business Plan. In flying you need a Flight Plan. At home you need a Budget and financial goals that includes God, a savings and investment strategy. These written plans help keep you purpose driven and guard against times of uncertainty.

BUSINESS PLAN

A Business plan is an effective means of defining goals and the steps needed to reach them. It spells out your purpose, vision and means of operation. It serves as your company's resume, explaining your objectives to investors, partners, employees, and vendors. It provides direction. The Christian Business plan should include all of the above plus it must model love, joy, peace, forbearance, kindness, goodness, fruitfulness, gentleness, and self-control.

FLIGHT PLAN

A Flight Plan is required by the Federal Aviation Administration for every flight. Once the company begins the initial implementation of the flight plan, the pilot **(Vision Chaser)** must "Vector" or adjust their plan to circumstances in order to ensure that they arrive at the final destination.

FAMILY BUDGET

A Budget is needed at home to make certain that bills get paid on time and funds are saved for goals and emergencies...etc. A budget is a plan to deal with money coming into a household and how that money is spent or invested over a certain period of time. Usually monthly or yearly.

WRITE THE VISION

Vision Chasers must have a written Vision. Have you ever tried to chase something you can't, see? Chasing becomes so much more effective if you can visualize your target. Writing provides clarity of thought and process. Thus, the vision must be written as the Word of God demands. God knew what he was instructing through Habakkuk. Habakkuk's message wasn't a military or social message, it wasn't political or philosophical, or an educational message-it was spiritual vision—and God told him to write it down, so he could remember it later. Not only did the vision have to be written, but it had to be plain. In other words, it had to be clear and easy to understand. The vision was written because God wanted His message to be permanent. That's why in business we insist on contracts, that things be written in black and white. Because we want to be able to hold people accountable. God wants His word to be permanent and He wants to be held to his word. He said, "My word will not return void!"

The Vision has to be written, it has to be plain, and it is also to be run with. It is to be chased and pursued. **Verse 2**: "Write the vision, and make it plain upon tables, that he may run that readeth it." It is to be read challengingly. It is to be pursued and chased afterwards. It is a message that when someone read it, it could be internalized, remembered, and pursued.

Writing and running with the Vision requires for you to put your faith on trial. As you write, you are affirming that God will provide what you have written. When you write the Vision you are demanding that God challenge, change, make, mold, deliver, shape, break you, and whatever else is needed to accomplish that which has been written. When you write and run with the vision, you are giving God praise in advance. **You are telling God that His credit is good with you while asserting yourself to the world that failure is not an option.**

We live in perplex and challenging times. We struggle in ways that our forefathers could not even imagine. The implications of the Covid 19 pandemic on our lives and our economy is unprecedented. Our lives have been put on pause as we deal with the difficulty of delayed gratification. We had become accustomed to everything must be now. Immediate gratification, fast, and my way. But when you write the vision, you are proclaiming that even if the vision is slow, your feet will never stop moving forward. Even in the midst of a pandemic we must keep our eyes on God. We might have some setbacks. We might go through a few crises, but they should not deter us from Chasing the Vision. The Angel carrying your blessing might get delayed—like he did for Daniel, but if you have written down the Vision, you will find courage to keep moving forward to receive your crown. Horses need blinders to keep them from being distracted by obstacles around them. Vision Chasers need a written version of the vision so they can stay focused during trying and frustrating time. If you have a potted plant in your home, notice that it is drawn to natural light. The plant will be drawn to the light so much so, that it will bend to reach it. That is why we must faithfully turn it every couple of days so it can grow. That's what a vision statement offers us...it's the light that draws us toward the fulfilment of the Vision.

So, the question is: "Do you have a unique vision as a church, business or individual?" Is it written clearly and concisely so that when you have what someone would call "an elevator speech moment", you can recall it easily and speak simply? Following a written vision allows you to still be fruitful even during frustrating times of a global pandemic. **Proverbs 29:18** states: "Where there is no vision, the people perish." Do you know the vision, God's dream and plan for your life, your ministry, your business, your family, your community, your state, country, the world? **Jeremiah 29:11** "For I know the plans I have for you, says the Lord, "plans to prosper you and not to harm to you, plan to give you hope and a future."

If the vision is slow, if it tarries wait for it, it will surely come. Martin Luther King, Jr. commented about the implications of dreaming God's dream, God's Vision.

How Long? NOT LONG, because no lie can live forever.

How Long? NOT LONG, because you still reap what you sow.

How Long? NOT LONG, because the arm of the moral universe is long, but it bends toward justice.

How Long? NOT LONG, "Cause my eyes have seen the glory of the coming of the Lord."

The dream, the growth of the business, the Vision tarries because it contains unfinished business. When God gives us a vision, it means we have inherited an ongoing struggle to pursue peace, happiness, equality, and **salvation for all.** It is the force inside of you that causes you to wake up every morning and say how can I grow today? That is why we are called Vision Chasers.

In order to chase the Vision, the vision must be well written. It must include key components. For example, a good vision statement must:

(1) Be written in the present, not in the future tense using unequivocal clear and concise language.

(2) It should inspire, be full of passion, and energize you, your subordinates, your colleagues, stakeholders, members, etc.

(3) It should build a picture, the same picture in the minds of people who read it.

(4) Although written in the present tense, it Projects 5 to 10 years into the future.

(5) It should describe what success looks like in your operation or life.

(6) It should contain measurable goals and outcomes.

When your vision statement is read, it should tell you where you are going like a GPS that will re-route and re-calculate to make sure you stay on course. It should be what you return to when life knocks you down.

I have never opened a business or started a ministry without a vision statement. In fact, the vision for the church my wife and I planted in 2009 reads as follows:

We Decree that people are standing in line to get into this church to hear the word of God. Every seat is filled in every service. Sunday morning service at 10:00am, Wednesday night Bible study at 7pm, noon Bible study on Tuesdays and any other service we might have. Everywhere our feet shall tread, we shall possess. Every need in this ministry is met and we are 100% tithers and payers. For this is a prosperous

year for us. All of our property is paid off in full and we owe nothing to no man-but to love him. Every member of this church is SAVED, healed, healthy, delivered, blessed and prosperous and we are reaching the world with the gospel, with our prayers and support. The doors of success are open. We shall succeed in everything in Christ. The doors of failure have been closed. We shall not know defeat. And we are fully persuaded that what God has promised, He is able to perform in Jesus' name. Amen!

We quoted it during every Sunday morning service and used it as our guiding light for every ministry implemented and every act of outreach and evangelism in our community. When attendance was low, we recited our vision, when the house was full, we recited our vision. When the devil attacked us, we recited our vision. No matter what the trial, test, or tribulation, we held on to the vision so we could stay focused and committed. When the Vision is clear, the people can always move forward. If we're motivated enough, we'll do whatever it takes to achieve our goals. What things are at the top of your list of things to persistently pursue? Have you written them down?

CHASING THE VISION

Once the Vision has been written it can be pursued by those who are called of God. Being a visionary is a divine vocation. **Visionaries** are called, not hired. **Your calling is for service. Not for status. Isaiah 42:6** states: "I the Lord have called thee!" When Paul discussed the ministry of reconciliation, he uses the term "Ambassadors" for Christ. I am an **Ambassador**. I am a friend of Jesus Christ. I have been justified **(declared righteous).** I am united with the Lord, and I am one with Him in Spirit. **1 Corinthians 6:19-20** I have been brought with a price and I belong to God. A **Torch Bearer** is someone who puts others before themselves. **Torch Bearers** change people's lives for the better wherever they travel in life. **Matthew 22:14**...." For many are called, but few are chosen." You cannot chase the vision on a whim or a desire. You must know that you have been called and chosen. Vision Chasers without a sure and sustaining call will one day become dropouts when the pressures of life mount. However, one can persevere over challenges when you know that you have been called and chosen. A calling, according to Merriam Webster, is a "a strong inner impulse toward a particular course of action, especially when accompanied by conviction of divine influence." A calling is magnetic. It draws you; it consumes you and drives your everyday life. **Your calling is an opportunity to show up and be you.** It's your opportunity to leave your mark on the world by impacting lives. Oliver Wendell Holmes stated: "Every calling is great when greatly pursued." You cannot fulfill a vision or a call if you don't know you have one. So, seek God's direction and find out what you are called to do. Being a Vision Chaser means you are a part of something bigger than yourself.... You are a part of God's plan.

Once you are called and chosen, you must chase and go the distance. **Chasing** is the act of pursuing someone or something. **Vision** is a discovery of God's plan for your life. **Vision** is foresight with insight. **Vision** is beginning a thing with the end in mind. **Vision** is the whole essence of your living. The reason you are sent into the world by God is for you to answer His call and fulfill a vision. When you get vision, it changes people's vision of you.

Vision is not the same as ambition. While ambition is what a man desires to become in life, vision is what God created him to become. The only meeting point of the two is where the will of a man is lost in the will of God. I have met a lot of ambitious people in my fifty-three (53) years of living. But I declare that Vision is higher than ambition. To become truly successful in life, your vision must become your ambition.

Nothing is greater than to know you been called and chosen by God to do something special for the Kingdom of God. However, being called by God to do something special, doesn't make you special. It makes you two things: a servant to God and a target of the enemy. People called and chosen by God to do something special have difficult lives. But their lives leave a lasting impression on those impacted by the fulfillment of the vision. For example, Abraham was called by God to be the Father of many nations. **Genesis 12:1** *"the LORD had said to Abram, "Go from your country, your people and your father's household to the land*

I will show you." To this day, Abraham is known as the Father of the Christian faith, but he had to walk away from all he knew and loved to become that. Moses was called by God to deliver the Israelites out of bondage from Egypt. **Exodus 3:4 When the LORD saw that he had gone over to look, God called to him from within the bush, "Moses! Moses!" And Moses said, "Here I am."** Gideon the farmer was called to be God's general. **Judges 6:12. When the angel of the LORD appeared to Gideon, he said, "The LORD is with you, mighty warrior."** Isaiah was called in a dream where he saw the throne room of God and heard God speak. **Isaiah 6:1 "In the year that King Uzziah died, I saw the Lord, high and exalted, seated on a throne; and the train of his robe filled the temple."** In **Mathew 4:18-22** Jesus calls Peter, Andrew, James, and John. In **verse 19,** *"Jesus said to them, Follow Me. I will make you fish for men!"* Jesus called them. Jesus promised them, and they followed. They all chose to chase after something bigger than themselves. Something bigger than their mistakes, misfortune, scars, and sins of their past. They followed God on nothing more than a call and a promise. Whatever, you are chasing must be your #1 priority. It must consume you and increase your faith because *y**ou are called to impact the lives of God's people.**

RECEIVING A VISION

How does one receive a Vision? A vision can be received in many different ways. The call is not diminished by the way it is delivered to us. Peter, Andrew, James, and John were called by God in Flesh. He was physically present and made an audible call. For you, it may have come while hearing a sermon, or during meditation and prayer. You may receive a vision simply because of status such as being the head of your household. Daily work or volunteer activities may have been the way God is leading you to your call. When you have been called, know that God is always present. He is aware of us even though we're not always aware of Him. Our God is omnipresent and omniscient. He knows us personally. It is His desire to walk with each one of us on this journey, as we pursue the calling given to us in the vision. If the visionaries of the past could do it, we can do it. We can sell out to God completely because we have more evidence of God than they did. We have over 2000 years of testimony of who God is. We have 66 books in the Bible and so much more. Therefore, when faced with troubles and trials in life, business, or ministry, we cannot forget our history with God or that He called you to Chase the Vision.

As we navigate through global uncertainty, never forget who called you? **2 Timothy 1:9 (ESV)** "Who saved us and called us to a holy calling, not because of our works but because of his own purpose and grace, which he gave us in Christ Jesus before the ages began." **Matthew 22:14 (ESV)** "for many are called, but few are chosen." **You are a rare flower and flowers don't pick themselves.** 1 Corinthian7:17 **(ESV)** "Only let each person lead the life that the Lord has assigned to him, and to which God has called him. This is my rule in all the churches." It is important to realize that we are all called by God. Paul writes, encouraging everyone, "I urge you to live a life worthy of the calling you have received." **(Eph. 4:1).** God made us with an inbuilt need for purpose. God called each of us to be servants and to be witnesses. **A witness (an Ambassador) is one who testifies.** We are called to testify of what we know about Jesus.

WHO ARE YOU?

God has already prepared the way. He's just preparing you. Once you have the vision (Mission statement, Business Plan, Family Budget) written down, there are several things you must know about yourself and the people you will encounter if you are to be successful. First, you must believe that you have been called and chosen to be a Vision Chaser. You must believe that you are a witness and servant of God. Just like Jesus asked the man who was possessed with Legion, God is asking who are you? Why? Because we are easily identified by the spirit that is within us. *You shall know them by the fruit of their spirit.* **Matthew 7:16.** Knowing who you are and how you see yourself determines your identity. **"The most important days in your life are the day you were born and the day you find out why." Mark Twain.** When you know who you are it determines your behavior. This is an important lesson for Vision Chasers because, while vision is cast on the outside, it starts from within. Too often we see ourselves as something less than who God tells us we are. All of life flows out of this issue of our primary identity with God or the lack of that identity. It makes a great difference if you see yourself only as a sinner or if you see yourself as a forgiven, new creation, a child of God.

How do you see yourself? Are you a lender or a borrower? Are you an owner or an employee?" *How great is the love the Father has lavished on us, that we should be called the children of God! And that is what we are! …. Dear friends, now we are the children of God...."* **(I John 3:1,2).** *"We are God's workmanship, created in Christ Jesus..."* **(Eph. 2:10).** Like the theme in my first book, **"X-Man: God's New Creature"**, *"Therefore, if anyone is in Christ, he is a new creation; the old has gone, the new has come!"* **(2 Cor. 5:17).** Can you honestly say, I know who I am?

Identity is important to Vision Chasers. God has identified you because He called you. So, are you a Visionary, an Ambassador, or a Torch Bearer? Do you know who your enemies are? In Business, Ministry and Life do you spend time studying your competition? In the fight for our souls, God has identified our enemy, Satan for who he is so you would recognize him. Satan tries to steal our identity. Jesus said in **John 10:10** that Satan's purpose is to steal, kill and destroy. He is the prince of this world. He is the Dragon, that ancient serpent. He is a liar and the father of lies. He is a deceiver. He is like a roaring lion seeking whom he may devour. Once you have been called and chosen of God, Satan is going to keep chasing you to try to steal your identity. If Satan can steal your identity, he can steal your purpose and vision. If he gets you to forget who you are, then you will be powerless and defeated. When God transforms you from the inside-out, not everybody will be happy and celebrate with you—especially the devil. When God sets you apart, your haters are going to show up because the ***more you chase the Vision, the more the enemy is going to chase you***. That's why you must never forget who you are or whose you are.

In life we call ourselves Christians because it identifies us with Christ. In business we market ourselves and our brand because it is what identifies us. You must promote yourself as a trusted Christian Business. You must grow your business without compromising your faith. Just because you are a Christian Business owner doesn't mean that God is just going to send you clients and customers. We must use tools like radio, newspapers, Television and Social media. Promotion is the key. For example:

- Advertise your business for free on Yelp, Waze, Google, etc.
- Take part in events and make your presence known
- Invite your non-believing friends and relatives
- Use emojis in Facebook ads to get more clicks-to make both an emotional and religious appeal to people
- Create a useful website
- Develop a referral program
- Develop a partnership with other local businesses and join your local chamber of commerce

Just like you promote your business, you must also promote what you believe spiritually. Spiritually, you and I get our identity from what Jesus did on Calvary. Calvary should be the motivation, the engine, the fuel for all that we are and all that we do. The greatest discovery that a person could make, is *self*-discovery. It is possible for a person to be born again, spirit filled, sanctified, speak in tongues, be a minister, teacher, apostle, prophet, bishop, pastor, deacon, or evangelist, without truly knowing who they really are. Often times the reason the devil is able to attack and trap us in sin is because we have forgotten who we are. Therefore, the lesson of identity is always important and necessary. For without the knowledge of your identity and the identity of your God, you are unable to stand in your proper place of destiny.

You know the identity of the devil, but you must also know the identity of Jesus? **Matthew 16:13-17**. We can't know who we are if we don't know who Jesus is. We need to be able to answer the way Peter did, "Thou are the Christ." Peter understood that Jesus was God in the flesh, the Savior, the Creator, the Sustainer, the Son of the Living God. We must believe the Nine (9) **I AM** statements of God and Jesus. 1. God told Moses; tell them I am that I am. 2. Jesus said, I am the way. 3. I am the truth. 4. I am the light. 5. I am the Bread. 6. I am the Good Shepherd. 7. I am the true vine. 8. I am the gate. 9. I am the resurrection and the life. Until you know fully who He is, there will always be some confusion about who you are. God tells me I am "fearfully and wonderfully made." **Psalm 139:14.** You are not just a Christian who happens to hold an office at your Church, serve as head of a ministry, operates a local business, or head up your household, but depending on setting you are a Visionary, an Ambassador or Torch Bearer.

There will clearly be times in business, life, and ministry that you will doubt who you are, whose you are, and your destiny. When we are confused about who we are, we can become convinced that we are insignificant and unimportant. We don't have a sense of belonging and purpose. Life becomes a burden as we are weighed down with stress and anxiety. The devil will attempt to identify you by your character flaws, your issues, and sins. When those times come, you need to remember that you are victorious. Stand on Victory and declare, "I shall not be moved!" You are new. *"For if any man, be in Christ he is a new creature. Old things are passed away, behold all things become new."* **(2 Cor. 5:17).** When you truly love God and follow Him, He gives you a new heart, a new mind, an ability to love people in spite of themselves. When life hits you hard, you need to remember that you are fearfully and wonderfully made in the likeness of your heavenly father. **Psalm 139:14.** When you think God is being silent in your situation, you need to remember that you are heard, and the **teacher never talks when the test is going on.** When you pray, your heavenly father hears you and He answers you. In this life, you will suffer persecution. "For I consider that the suffering of this present time is not worthy to be compared with the Glory which shall be revealed in us." **Romans 8:18**. You must know the truth. Ye shall know the truth and the truth shall make you free. The scripture does not say you must **have** the truth, but that you must **know** the truth. Because you can have the truth and still not know it. You can have the Word of God in your hand and still not have it in your heart and spirit. You can have your vision, mission statement, family budget, business plan written down and posted on the walls and still not have it in your spirit.

Because you are called and chosen by God, the devil will use people to question who you are in Christ and highlight your inexperience. They will bring up your past and try to tie it to your present. They will put you down in order to lift themselves up. **John 15: 18-22** *"If the world hates you, keep in mind that it hated me first. If you belonged to the world, it would love you as its own. As it is, you do not belong to the world, but I have chosen you out of the world. That is why the world hates you."* **When the devil keeps on asking you to look at your past, that means that there is something good in the future he doesn't want you to see.**

As a Vision Chaser, being hated and targeted by people can be hard to digest, especially if you don't know who you are. **1 John 3:10** tells us, *'this is how we know who the children of God are and who the children of the devil are: Anyone who does not do what is right is not a child of God; nor is anyone who does not love his brother.'* This is the only test needed to show our true character. In

2nd Corinthians 13:5, Paul instructs us to, '*examine yourselves to see whether you are in the faith; test yourselves. Do you not realize that Christ Jesus is in you--unless, of course, you fail the test?*' So **"Vision Chaser",** when was the last time you examined yourself to see who you are? Does your business plan, family budget, marketing strategy, etc. include God?

Your destiny is waiting. Let us not find ourselves as indecisive as Alice is in Lewis Carroll's classic *Alice's Adventures in Wonderland.* You will remember that she comes to a crossroads with two paths before her, each stretching onward but in opposite directions. She is confronted by the Cheshire cat, of whom Alice asks, "Which path shall I follow?" The cat answers, "That depends on where you want to go. If you do not know where you want to go, it doesn't matter which path you take." Unlike Alice, we all know where we want to go because we have written our vision, our mission our business plan down, and family budget for such a time as this. Having our vision constantly before us is needed because decisions are constantly before us. To make them wisely, courage is needed—the courage to say no, the courage to say yes because **Decisions Determine Destiny.**

Whenever the enemy rises up against you, you need to remember who you are. I know it's been a few years, but you should see the movie "**Black Panthe**r" Wahanda Forever. When T'Challa, the Black Panther's father is killed, T'Challa now ascends to the throne. Before he can take the throne; however, he must go through a challenge. You cannot get to a throne unless you get through some challenges. You cannot expect to realize the Vision without experiencing some challenges. T'Challa is challenged by M'Baku. M'Baku is beating up on T'Challa. T'Challa is bleeding from his nose, and he is in a choke hold by M'Baku. It looks as if T'Challa is beaten. But then his mother, Ramondo, played by Angela Bassett, yells out: "**Show them who you are!**" T'Challa then says, "I am T'Challa son of T'Chaka and that's when victory came. It wasn't until he recognized who he was that he had the strength to defeat his enemy. You and I are the sons and daughters of God almighty. It's time we remember and declare who we are.

Every day that you withstand the challenges of the enemy and pursue the vision, you are showing the devil and his minions who you are! Being a successful Christian Business is not a contradiction or oxymoron if you continue following God-- prosperity will come. Because you are the light of the world. You are the salt of the earth. You are a child of the king. You are a Visionary, an Ambassador, or a Torch Bearer. You are more than a conqueror in Christ Jesus. When you know who you are, you can tell the devil: I don't need you in my life. By letting the enemy know who you are, you are also letting them know who your Father is. Call out His names. There is power in the name of Jesus: the name above every name. Heart fixer, mind regulator, burden bearer, heavy load sharer, rock in a weary land, shelter in times of storm, water when thirsty, bread when you are hungry, doctor when you are sick, counselor when you are stressed. There is something about that name: Yahweh, Elohim, JESUS, Rose of Sharon, Lilly of the Valley, Bright and Morning Star, Adam's redeemer, Cain's vindicator, Moses Rod, Ezekiel's wheel, Joseph's dream, Jacob's ladder. The name that lifts burdens and breaks chains. If you ever want to change the situation or the atmosphere in the room—just show them who you are and call on the name of JESUS! Say His name, Say His name.

Isaiah 9:6 states unto us a child is born. Unto us a son is given. And the government will be upon His shoulders. And His name shall be called wonderful counselor, mighty God, everlasting father, prince of peace. If you know who you are, you should be proclaiming the name of Jesus. In 1999, "Destiny's Child" came out with a song written by Beyoncé' that says: "say my name, say my name. If you ain't running game, then say my name." When you need relief from the burdens of life and ministry. Just go and sit still for a moment and say our Savior's name. Say His name, say His name. The name of God can bring success out of struggle, triumph out of tribulation and tragedy. God can create destiny out of dysfunction.

So don't you dare quit. If you need strength to go on, just scream the name of Jesus. Some would say that the Church quit and raised the white flag long before the pandemic when we surrendered our voice to preach, teach and practice true biblical doctrine. We imposed our own kind of self-quarantine by limiting what we preach, teach, and pray publicly—as not to offend or convict sinners to repent. You can't turn your back on God and the people of God. Social distancing is necessary. Relational distancing is not. Vision is seeing the coronavirus not just as a plague, but as an invitation to know God. It's an opportunity for us to recognize the sovereignty of God over creation and our lives. So, be steadfast because you never know when God is going to turn things around. You don't know when God is going to bring restoration. Your little light is about to shine again. You are about to go from depression to deliverance. All you have to do is start to call on Jesus. Say His name. Say His name. **America needs to say his Name!**

We all go through things. For some of us, had we not known the name of Jesus, we would have lost our mind. As we continue to endure this pandemic, America needs to take a step back, call on His name for healing, repentance, and deliverance. When you call God by name—there is no limit to who God is and what He can do. He told Moses, tell them "I Am that I Am." He asked His disciples who do men say that I am.

Matthew 16:13-16, *"When Jesus came into the coast of Caesarea Philippi, he asked his disciples, saying, whom do men say that I the Son of man am? And they said, some say that thou art John the Baptist: some Elias, and others, Jeremias, or one of the prophets. He saith unto them, but who say ye that I am? And Simon Peter answered and said, Thou art the Christ, the Son of the living God."* He is the Christ that can lift your burdens, heal your bitterness and internal pain. No matter how many pieces it has been broken into, our Mighty God can mend your marriage and restore relationships. As a Mighty God, He can help raise your children. He can open doors for you—that no one can close. He can close doors—that nobody can open. He's a mighty God, miracle worker, and light in the darkness. Which name are you going to call Him? I ask because our God can be everything at the same time. So, rise, shine for your time has come to call on the name of Jesus.

Abraham was on mount Moriah with his son Isaac getting ready for the sacrifice when God spoke and placed a ram in the bush. After that, Abraham started calling God, Jehovah Jireh—the God who provides. The experience he went through showed him a characteristic of God he had not known before. The three (3) Hebrew boys went through the furnace experience. God Himself got in the fire with them and delivered them. They started calling God, Jehovah Shammah, the God who is there. Somebody was sick when God healed them, and they called Him Jehovah Rapha—the

God who heals. Don't get discouraged. God is giving you a "Vision Chasing Experience" that, when you come out of it, you will have a new revelation of who God is. And if you have a new revelation of who God is, that means you also have a new revelation of the power, influence, character, and nature of God working on the inside of you.

I dare you to just call His name. Say His name, Say His name. Even in the midst of a pandemic whosoever shall call upon the name of the Lord shall be saved. Because at the name of Jesus, every knee shall bow, every tongue shall confess to the glory of God that Jesus is Lord. **Know who you are so you can show them who you are! His name is at the foundation of our faith. His name and His Kingdom is what we promote in our role as Visionary, Ambassador or Torch Bearer.**

YOU ARE A VISION CHASER

Unless you are confident in who you are, navigating your way through life when it comes to Ministry, leading your Family or operating a Christian Business is like walking through a minefield. But you are a Vision Chaser! You were created to standout, to be extraordinary. You are not mainstream. You are unstoppable. **Vision Chasers don't wait for the right opportunity, they create it.** Because God the creator lives on the inside of you. You have been blessed with the ability to imagine and create. Ross Caligiuri stated: "If you feel like you don't fit into the world you inherited, it is because you were born to help create a new one." Robert Frost stated: "Two roads diverged in a yellow wood and I- I took the one less traveled by, and that has made all the difference." Vision Chasers always travel the road less traveled.

1 Timothy 6:11 and **2 Timothy 3:1-14** contains a lot of verses starting out with **But you...But you** are different. **But you** are set apart. **But you** have been called out. There are times when you are in ministry, and you wish you could deal with or handle things the same way the world would handle them. In 2013 a movie titled "The Purge" came out. The Purge is based on a future dystopian America where once a year for twelve (12) hours all crime-including murder is made legal. I know in my flesh I wanted a purge day, where God would allow me an opportunity to deal with a few of my enemies in an ungodly manner. When I would finish, I could just return back into His arms. But because I am a believer, I keep hearing those words-**But You!** But you can't do what everyone else does. But you can't deal with people in your flesh. But you—will have consequences when you sin. But you have been set apart.

Sometimes when the rubber really hits the road, you wrestle with decisions: do I do what I want to, or do I do what God wants me to do? Do I do what people expect for me to do or do I do what God expects of me? **Just because people are speaking from a good place and have great ideas—doesn't necessarily mean that what they are suggesting is the will of God.** When you are "Chasing the Vision", you are giving God the right to step in between what you want and what He wants. God says, But You! I know you want to start and restart somethings, but you. I know you want to act and react like other people at work, but you! I know you want to cut up and walk in your flesh—But You! I know you helped give that child life but today you want to choke the life out of them—But you! I know the relationship isn't always what you would like it to be, and you thought about walking out and giving up-But you!

When I was growing up my parents were very strict. I remember trying to negotiate for a later curfew. It was an exercise in futility. I had to be in the house when the streetlight came on. My mother would say, "you dark skin, you've been touched by the sun." So, when the sun was no longer out—I couldn't be out either. But I had my argument ready. I began to tell my parents about the liberties of some of my friends who could stay out later. Bobby didn't have to be home until 8pm. Danny could go home whenever he got ready. My mother flung her house coat to the side, put her hands on her hip, and pointed her finger at me and said, "I don't care what Bobby and Danny do. They don't live here. I don't care how late they get to stay out—**but you** better be home before them streetlights come on. I asked why? She responded –because you gone come into this house when I tell you to. Because there is a difference between you and them. You belong to me. I am responsible for you. I give you direction and instruction. When you are outside this house you don't represent Edward, you represent me and your father. In other words, I was an Ambassador for the Benson Family. I was the successor of my father. So, I couldn't be or do what others did, because of who I represented. Vision Chaser, God is saying you can't be like everyone else. You can't do what everyone else does. Because you belong to Him (His Visionary, His Ambassador and His future Torch Bearer) it's His responsibility to give you direction and instruction.

Paul had a very similar discussion with Timothy. I encourage you to read 1st and 2nd Timothy. Paul tells Timothy I know what's going on in the world. I know about the false teachers. I know about the believers who have back slid. I know about the unbelievers who cannot come to the light of Jesus Christ because they have been blinded by false teachings. I know about the left out and the forgotten. I know about those who have fallen away and are now doing their own thing. I know about those that know Christ but are still in need of deliverance from the hell that has consumed them. **BUT YOU**—cannot do what they do. You cannot say what they say. You have been set apart. You cannot live how they live. You cannot think how they think. You cannot go where they go. Because you have been called into a life of distinction. You are a "Vision Chaser". If you have been called to chase the vision of God, then God has placed a **"But You"** over your life. I know you will see people doing carnal things, living in sin, with no accountability and you start to think—well why can't I...Because you are different.

You have been Set Apart. If you are going to live this life of distinction and be a Vision Chaser there are few qualities, you need to have.

- You must have the right message.
- You must have the right mentors.
- You must have the right mindset.

RIGHT MESSAGE

2 Timothy 3:14 (NLT) says, **But you** must remain faithful to the things you have been taught. You must be faithful to the faith, faithful to the things that are true in Christ Jesus. Paul tells Timothy, but you know the truth. You know the truth and the people that taught you the truth. As a Vision Chaser you've got to keep the right message—because there are enough people preaching and teaching the wrong message. It's hard enough to chase the vision with this duality about us. But it's even harder when your mind has been twisted with false teaching and devilish noise.

RIGHT MENTOR

If you are going to chase the vision of ministry, business and lead your family in the ways of Jesus Christ then you need to have a physical Church, you can call home. A place where you can learn and grow. You need to pray: "God show me who I should be listening to and sitting under and when I have heard from everybody, let it flow through a filter, so I will know which part is from you—and which part is not." As you Chase the Vision, it is so critical to get the right message. As a vision chaser you can't believe every spirit because every spirit is not of God. God will always give you what and who you need in your life when you need them. In Ephesians 4:11 the scripture says, "so Christ himself gave some apostles, some prophets, some evangelist and some pastors and teachers." He gives us these people in our lives to build us up and to equip us for our calling. God gives us Mentors to help us mature. Mentorship takes an investment of time. How much time are you willing to invest to be mentored?

One Survey among pastors found that 70% do not have a close friend, confidant, or mentor. Godly mentors help you with your blind spots. Thus, don't allow someone to be an influence in your life that hasn't been sent by God. Don't let people walk up to you and tell you—God told me to cover you. Try the spirit by the spirit and see if it is of God. Where God is taking you, you need a friend and mentor for that season. You need an authentic anointed mentor sent by God whose life you know, like they know yours. *If you don't know their life and their walk in Christ—do not give that person, the right to speak into your life.* You do not have time for set-backs due to being mis-mentored. The wrong mentor will set you back and hold you back. It's hard to be a Vision Chaser if you've got the wrong mentor. The key to success and failure often times is who we take our cues from. As you continue to chase the vision be very careful about who is discipling you. Who is mentoring you? Who are you allowing to pour into your life and whisper in your ear?

Sometimes Vision Chasers either don't have a mentor or they stay in mentoring relationships past their season. Mentoring happens in seasons and at different levels. When the season is over—respectfully move on. You may need a different mentor during the Visionary stage of chasing the vision verses the Ambassador and Future Torch Bearer season. When the season is over, and the business has grown, or the spiritual level has changed—move on. Nobody wants to be in winter 365 days a year. When the season is over, write them a letter, take them out to lunch and thank them for all that they poured into you, but you must keep chasing the vision of God. You got a thirst for knowledge, wisdom and understanding that your current mentor is unable to provide. *Why keep drinking from a fountain that no longer quenches your thirst.* For example, I can teach my kids how to ride a bike. I can teach them how to drive. But if anyone of them wants to learn how to fly a plane—I'm not the guy for that. They can love me and keep hanging out with me. But if they are waiting on me to teach them how to fly, they are wasting their time. They need a pilot to instruct them because they are on another level.

Some of you need "pilot like mentoring," but you still talking to people on the ground. Mentoring happens on levels. There are people who are gifted at pre-school teaching and what they do is critical to the life-long development of that child. What they are doing in those formative years is critical. They are experts at preparing a child at the preschool level. But if you're in the 4th grade—still going to pre-school for instruction—you are retarding your growth. Listen, as you mature, your mentors and support system must mature also. Every level requires new mentorship.

RIGHT MINDSET

You have got to have the right message and the right mentor if you are to have the right mindset. If you don't have the right mind, you will become weak and fall away from the faith and give up your divine destiny. **2 Timothy 3:10 (NLT)** says, but you, Timothy, know my faith, my patience, my love, and my endurance. I know people have been misled by Jannis and Janbris, but you know my life, you know how I live. You know what I teach, you know my purpose. You know what I have endured. You know me. Paul was Timothy's mentor. **Paul was teaching Timothy how to become his Ambassador and Future Torch Bearer.** As a Vision Chaser, you need a mentor. **A mentor is someone you know.** Don't give someone that title in your life and you do not know them. As you move forward, and your seasons change, your mentor might need to change. You need a mentor that will help keep you humbled, hungry and honored to be a servant of God and grow as a Visionary, Ambassador or Future Torch Bearer.

In **1 Timothy 6:11** the text states: "But you, Timothy, are a man of God; so, run from all these evil things. Pursue righteousness and a godly life, along with faith, love, perseverance and gentleness." But you "Vision Chaser" are a man (woman) of God. You are not some ordinary person. Having that mindset is critical to living out this faith. To know that there is a **BUT YOU**—hovering over your life. It is critical to have the right mindset. Be ye transformed by the renewing of your mind. In a time where believers are going astray and backsliding it's imperative that you know **(But You)** are a child of the King.

Without the right mindset you will forget that you were set aside for a purpose. Without the right mindset, when life beats you down you will be ready to abandon everything you know to be right. You will be ready to leave the church. Leave your marriage. Ready to give up on the business plan. Ready to leave perfectly healthy relationships with friends and family, but God is saying – **BUT YOU.** I know you are tired, depressed, dissatisfied—But God is saying, **But you!** You are different, you are distinct, chosen and set apart. This is the mindset of Christ, and it must be your mindset as well. **Philippians 2:5** says let this mind be in you, which was also in Christ Jesus.

Our mindset must be to win in victory. If we are honest, the devil has won a few battles. But remember it was only a battle that you lost; it was not the war. The fight is still ongoing, and you will be more than victorious in Christ Jesus. In **1 Timothy 6:12** Paul tells Timothy that he has to have a fighter's mentality. You have to fight the good fight of faith. Every day, you will wrestle with demons, temptation and the flesh, and the reason you are in a constant fight is because you are a target. You are **public enemy number 1** according to Satan. But you can't punk out. You have got to be a fighter. **The devil is a bully. The only way you defeat a bully is you got to let the bully know you not scared.** It is time to fight. You have got to fight for your family. Fight for your marriage and your relationships. You have got to fight for your ministry and the divine vision God has called you to. You've got to fight for the integrity of your business as a Christian run company.

For the weapons of our warfare are not carnal but are mighty through God to the pulling down of strongholds. If you want to see the strong arm of God move on your behalf, you need to implement the Resurrection power of Jesus Christ. Our weapons are prayer, fasting, the word of God, praise, worship, church, fellowship. So, if you are determined to win this race, you need to get equipped and empowered to fight the demons that are determining to take you out of the chase. Because there are some people who are being used by the devil and ***they measure success in their life, by their ability to destroy yours.*** The devil (**your competitor**) is trying to defeat you, so you have got to fight back with the tools of God's word.

You can avoid some of the enemy's attacks simply by running, not out of fear but running toward your destiny. In **verse 11** Paul tell Timothy to run away from evil things and people. Some people you simply have to walk away from. You cannot stand still and let evil track you down and consume you. I know you are saying but why should I run if I am more than a conquer. Because in order to chase you must run. Every day you have to run the race of destiny that is set before you. You have to pray God give you the strength to keep chasing, to keep running to put some distance between your present and your past. You can't afford to slow down because, as sure as you are chasing the vision of God, the enemy is chasing you. You must pursue righteousness. The word pursue is stronger than run or chase. **Pursue** means to track down something; to hunt something down or to apprehend. You have to **pursue** the person you were created, called, and predestined to become. The eyes of heaven are upon you, waving the checkered flags in the distance. **KEEP CHASING!**

WAIT, REST & CHASE

A Pastor was telling a true story about an elderly couple in his church who loved each other very much. They epitomized the picture of the two becoming one. They had been married four (4) decades and then the elderly wife got sick and lapsed into a coma. Her husband was devastated. So much so that he goes to his Pastor, and they go and visit her at the hospital to pray for her, anoint her and lay hand on her for healing. Nevertheless, for six (6) months she remained in the coma—while they trusted, prayed, and believed God for her healing. Her husband became so depressed and disillusioned until he took his own life. One week after he commits suicide—his wife comes out of the coma. When the Pastor finished telling the story it clearly implied that had the husband waited on God for seven (7) more days, that things would have been different?

"Chasing the Vision" in ministry, family, and business is about developing a lifestyle of trusting and waiting on God. I know you're thinking the same as me—**waiting is the opposite of Chasing**. Chasing the Vision is about trusting God—even when you can't trace God steps. In order to chase, you must master the ability to rest and wait on God. In **Isaiah 40:31** the Prophet is seeking to get the children of God to learn how to wait on God. "But those who wait on the Lord, shall renew their strength, they shall mount up with wings like eagles. They shall run and not be weary—they shall walk and not faint." Isaiah is ministering to the Israelites after 70 years of bondage in Babylon. God had allowed the Israelites to be enslaved because of their sin and disobedience. God sought to disciple them for 70 years to bring them back to him.

Now that the Israelites are out of bondage, they are trying to rebuild their lives and community. But they are disillusioned and depressed. They are mad at God; they think that he doesn't love them. Some of us feel their pain for how God could love us and allow us to go through so much hell. Sometimes when you look at the road God has you on, you wonder if God remembers us or even if He truly cares. The Israelites are on the verge of giving up. With as much death and destruction as this coronavirus pandemic has caused, a lot of leaders, lay Christians, and business owners, may feel like giving up, stepping down or just flat out –quitting. How can it be that we are children of the most high God, and yet the devil seems to pluck us off one by one? Have you ever found yourself asking, "why is all this happening? How could a God be good and allow this stuff to happen? I'm not talking about just any old body. I'm talking about the Lord's people. I'm talking about the Bible fed, and spirit led. **How can God be God and we struggle as hard as we do.** We see heathens making it. We see atheist getting over. We see people that believe God, but not Jesus, making it. But the more we try to do right, the harder life seems to get. We ask ourselves where is God in this calamity? What is God up to—in my life?

After lockdown and quarantine and vaccines and the lifting of the restriction the COVID-19 cases continue to rise, it is clear that we don't have all the answers, but we must maintain our faith. We are still living in a country where we need to show God's love to people, to be a fragrance of Christ to those who have heard the good news. Zoom Chats, Facebook live, WhatsApp messages are not the same as a hug and the fellowship shared over a meal. Our God is not affected by the virus and His power is not limited by social distancing. In a mask-wearing, six-feet distance-keeping, COVID-19 world we must still chase the vision. Thus, we must master the ability to rest and wait on God. If you feel that there is really no answer for what you are going through—just wait and rest—God will reveal all things in time. Stay on course. Stay in the fight. Stay in Business. Stick to the Budget. **Go back and read the written vision.** God has a master plan. **Don't make any permanent decisions for your temporary problems.** When Job's wife told him to commit suicide—he said no, I'm going to wait until my change comes. *Chasing the Vision is about trusting God over time.*

When you study the Israelites –you get it. When I look back over my own life—I get it. When I see the effects of the pandemic in America, I get it. For the Israelites, they had been in a war, with one spiritual battle after another. The people were oppressed, suppressed, and depressed in Babylon when they longed to be back home in Israel. It's hurtful to see where you are in life—and know that is not where you should be. It's disheartening to consistently be mistreated and know deep down inside—you deserve to be treated better. Sometimes you have to take a step out of the ring because you are tired of fighting one battle after another—with no rest. Sometimes you just get sick and tired of being sick and tired. When this happens, know that there is nothing wrong with taking a break to hear from God for direction. Despite your current situation—remember that our God is able.

However, you got to your breaking point—Isaiah says: "But they that wait on the Lord." When the prophet saw all the depression and hopelessness, he asked the people to revisit their theology. **In order to have the strength to Chase, you must have the patience to wait. You cannot allow your sociology to shape your theology.** It doesn't' matter what you are facing, God can fix it. He can work it out. In **Isaiah 40:21** it states: "Do you not know? Have you not heard? Has it not been told you from the beginning? Have you not understood since the earth was founded?" Our God has no beginning or no end. He is Elohim—the creative God. He creates a way out of no way. There is no searching of God's understanding. Just because you don't understand God— doesn't mean God doesn't know what He's doing. **He gave you the Vision—trust Him to deliver on His promise. Philippians 1:6** states, "being confident of this, that he who began a good work in you will carry it on to completion until the day of Jesus Christ."

Our God is not a quitter. He gave you the vision that you are chasing. "And our God is not a man, that he should lie, neither the son of man, that he should repent: hath he spoken, and shall he not do it? Or hath he spoken, and shall he not make it good?" **Numbers 23:19.** Our God is faithful. He is constant and without change or repentance. Therefore, if our God is not a quitter and His spirit lives inside of you—then you are not a quitter. **It is not in your spiritual DNA.** Your Vision Chasing is about to take you in a different direction. It will cause you to go against the grain in Business and Ministry. **So, wait on the Lord—to give you strength for the race that is set before you.** No matter what lies ahead of you, God is already there. This race—this chase— requires waiting.

Just because you are impatient in other areas of your life—pray for patience with God. Learn to wait for strength for the Chase. **Habakkuk 2:3** For the vision is yet for an appointed time, but at the end it shall speak, and not lie **though it tarry, wait for it**; because it will surely come, it will not tarry." Wait on God with expectancy. Waiting on God is not a passive activity. Waiting on God actually serves as a time of preparation. When God answers we must be prepared for the answer.

We rest, but our God never stops working. The snow never stops being cold, rain never stops being wet and our God never stops being God. Yes, God rested from creation. But He kept working on salvation. He kept working on our liberation and emancipation. He kept working on sanctification. He kept working on glorification. He kept working things out for our good. That's why you and I should learn and practice resting in the grace of God, because God never stops working. He is available to handle things while we take a physical, spiritual, mental, and emotional break. God is working all things out for our good. Our God has no limits. Our God is always working.

In the Ten Commandments God commanded Israel to rest on the seventh day. A lot of visions go unfulfilled because visionaries are busy trying to work like God and fail to get the proper rest. A lot of people perish because they have never seen the impact of a vision. Vision Chasers are creators, and you must learn to not just wait on God, but rest from the work of the Vision God has called you to create. **A vision is life giving. But lack of rest will kill it.** We cannot allow anything, including mental, physical, or spiritual fatigue, to hinder us from doing our best, so rest!

These are perilous days, but they are the days we have. We can sit around like victims, or we can choose to "Chase the Vision." I know somebody is saying, I'm not just tired of waiting, but I'm just tired. **The kind of tired that sleep won't solve.** Such tiredness can cause you to lose your way—because ministry, family, the business, the organization has sucked the breath out of you. Tired. Tired of using your best efforts only to be beaten down, talked about, and ridiculed by some of the very people you helped the most.

Vision Chasers, you better rest up because you're going to take a daily beating in the pursuit of the Vision and you going to get snake bitten a few times. If you don't rest, you run the risk of becoming spiritually and mentally stuck. It's impossible to move forward when you are stuck. A few winters ago, after a heavy snowstorm, my family got up the next morning to shovel our way out. Notwithstanding our efforts, my daughter Tiffany's car was stuck in the mud. The car was covered in mud as I attempted to back the car up. The tires were spinning, but there was no movement. There is nothing like the feeling of having no control and little ability to get out of a situation. My son, Malik, and I had worked diligently to no avail. Finally, we took a rest which allowed us to get a different perspective of our dilemma. Once we got some rest, we came back and after a little more pushing and pulling and a little creative thinking of using some rocks and a piece of plywood, we were able to get out of the mess we were in. Sometimes we must realize that we are spiritually and mentally drained and stuck just like Tiffany's car. We are moving forward physically, but spiritually and mentally we are burned out and stuck.

Most people get stuck in financial difficulty, the job they hate, the unhealthy relationship, the addiction they can't quit, the effects of a pandemic. **WILL THIS PANDEMIC END! WILL NORMAL EVER RETURN!** We are physically, spiritually, and mentally stuck. Like I discussed in my book **"Holler Jesus"**, we are stuck spiritually like Bartimeaus was stuck in blindness or like conservatives get stuck in tradition. We get stuck in the mud of our own sin because we have lost the strength to keep pushing and pulling in prayer for deliverance, healing, or forgiveness. Our mindset will get stuck, and it is so easy to slip when you are trying to run in mud. Before you can move forward, you are going to need rest and restoration, strength, and a fresh perspective. Vision Chasers, it is great to be resilient. However, there will be set-backs and more work to be done—so rest. There will always be some turmoil and persecution, so rest.

Most people don't know how to rest and relax. They are Work Alcoholics feeding off the adrenaline of being busy. They are unable to enjoy anything they have worked for. They are always in a hurry. Their to-do list is unreasonably long, they use their day off to catch up on unfinished work, they are always having people tell them to slow down. They feel guilty when they relax, and they **have to get sick to really get time off**. Does this sound like you? You need to know that God considers rest just as important as work. You have to learn how to balance life. Don't become exhausted because you are trying to hurry God or trying to be all things to all people. **Exodus 23:29-30 King James Version (KJV) 29** "I will not drive them out from before thee in one year; lest the land become desolate, and the beast of the field multiply against thee. **30 By little and little** I will drive them out from before thee, until thou be increased, and inherit the land." People could relax more if they understood that God has a plan. **His plan is to grow you little by little.** While God is growing your Ministry, He is also growing you. While He is growing your Business, He is also growing you. While God is growing your Children and your Career, He is also growing you. Learn to rest in God's grace so that you can handle the demands of Chasing the Vision. Your lack of rest and waiting on God will affect every area of your life. Ministry, operating a business, or leading a family is hard enough with rest. Imagine the repercussions if the Visionary does not get rest?

Rest is a break from our routine, it is doing something that is rejuvenating and mentally relaxing including sleeping. Even a small amount of sleep deprivation takes a significant toll on our health, mood, cognitive capacity, and productivity. It diminishes concentration, impairs memory, reduces the ability to communicate, lowers creativity, triggers moodiness, and increases stress. Sleep deprivation can hold you back rather than propel you forward. Most high performing executives fail to get enough sleep. As a Vision Chaser you can sacrifice a lot of things, but sleep cannot be one of them. Rest allows you to maintain your **zeal for ministry.**

Contrary to popular opinion, Vision Chasers are not superheroes. You are not invincible to the effect of the attacks of the enemy. You are a wounded warrior who when hit with the enemies best, still gets up and give God praise. It doesn't matter how spiritually strong you are, you must rest. And let some things go. Chasing the Vision is **a life of service to God.** But as life goes forward there are some things you must let go of in order to grab hold to something new. There are things in your life and in your spirit, that if you don't learn to let go, they will be the death of your ministry, your business, family, finances, and the death of you. I remember watching a documentary on National Geographic about a bald eagle that had a 7ft wingspan. They were watching and observing the Eagle in its natural habitat. The Eagle got hungry and flew down into the lake and came up with a great fish. The fish was heavy, and the Eagle was having trouble flying with the heavy fish in its talons. The eagle tried to rise but couldn't. He tried to unlock his talons, but he had dug in too deep. He was trying to shake it off but couldn't. An Eagle has an innate ability to rise high, but he's not able to do it, because he's locked on to something that is pulling him down. The camera man and others continued to observe and watch the struggle of the Eagle all while screaming, why won't it just let the fish go. After several minutes of struggling with the fish, the eagle was observed drowning. The Eagle drowned because it couldn't or wouldn't let go? There was no deliverance for the Eagle, but there is deliverance for you and me if we just know when to let go. Don't be afraid to let things go, if even for a little while. If you lack the strength to carry on—let it go. **When you don't have enough strength to handle yesterday's pain. Let It Go!**

If you've ever watched the Indy 500, you know that no one wins the race without making **pit stops**. Pit stops allow the tires to be changed, adjustments to be made, the tank to be refueled, and other necessary mid-Race adjustments to be made to finish the race strong. Rest, because quitting is not an option. Rest in God and get some spiritual oxygen and take some deep breaths in Christ, because your journey is just beginning. This is not a sprint; it is a marathon. Rest – because the snakes and the noise are coming.

Venom & Vision

Genesis 3:1 (NIV) "Now the serpent was craftier than any of the wild animals the Lord God had made..." Twice in Revelations, (12:9;20:2) Satan is called that "old serpent." **Beware of snakes.** The problem is not like the movie with Samuel L. Jackson, "Snakes on A Plane." Where hundreds of snakes were released on a passenger plane in an attempt to kill a trial witness. The problem is snakes in business, the Church, in ministry and even in families. If you are a Vision Chaser you have a spiritual enemy, and he is called a snake. We don't go out looking for snakes! But I assure you that if you chase the Vision God has given you, you will encounter snakes, or the snakes will come looking for you.

If you chase the vision the venomous snakes are going to attack. As a Vision Chaser you need spiritual discernment of snakes disguised as people. If you don't learn how to discern the snakes, you will get bitten every time. Growing up in Mississippi, my daddy would always tell us remember...**a snake is a snake**. There are 2900 species of snakes in this world. And they range in size from 4" to 30' in length. They come in all colors, and they come poisonous and non-poisonous. But I don't care if it is only 4" long and it's as beautiful as a rainbow, a snake is a snake. The devil comes in all shapes and sizes too. Sometimes he comes in typical form and fashion and sometimes he comes as an angel of light. Sometimes he comes loud and other times he comes silent. Sometimes he comes boldly and other times he comes sneaky. Sometimes he comes in like a flood and other times he comes in like a soft summer breeze. But what we have to remember is whenever he comes and whatever shape he comes in, a snake is a snake. I don't care if a person wraps himself up in education and calls himself a professor. If he challenges the divinity of Jesus Christ and tries to make you doubt God... a snake is a snake. If you are running a business and they are trying to sabotage you—a snake is a snake. She might be a beautiful woman with a pleasing personality. But if she tries to come in between you and your wife, a snake is a snake. They might seem like harmless friends and they're for sure fun to hang around, but when they start pulling you in a different direction than what you know is right.... You better look around because there's a snake **(a sabotage)** hissing in the shadows.

I remembered reading a story about an Indian warrior who climbed to the top of a mountain. When he got to the top, it was snowing and cold. But he noticed a rattle snake. The rattle snake spoke to the warrior. The snake asked, could you pick me up and take me down into the valley where it is warm. If I stay up here, I will die. The warrior stated, "but if I pick you up, you will bite and kill me. "The snake promised the warrior, "if you help me, protect me, cover me and keep me warm, I will not bite you." The warrior feeling compassion, reached down, and picked up the snake, put it inside of his coat to keep warn until he reached the bottom of the hill. Once the warrior had arrived in the valley, he took the snake out of his coat and placed it on the warm ground. Immediately, the rattle snake curled up and, without hesitation, bit the warrior. The warrior exclaimed, "you promised if I helped you, you would not bite me." The snake responded, yes, "**but you knew I was a snake when you picked me up.**"

In **Genesis 3** Adam had a moment when he encountered Satan (the serpent) in the garden. But when he refused to take authority over the serpent, he placed himself in a reactive position instead of a proactive position. In other words, he refused to attack an enemy and because he refused to attack, he found himself reacting to an attack and it cost him and all of creation dearly. You must always be on the lookout for attacks coming against your business, your ministry, your family, and God's vision. **Today God is saying... recognize who your enemy is and call a snake a snake.**

Beware of those with a serpent spirit whose sole objective is to tempt, mislead and destroy you. To do this, you need discernment. To discern properly, you need to be rested enough that you can hear from the Holy Spirit. If you have the spirit of discernment instead of picking up the snake you will take authority over the serpent. Discernment is key because some snakes wear Clergy attire, others have the right titles such as Deacon, Apostle, Prophet, Elder, Reverend, Pastor, and Teacher, while others have cute smiles and say all of the right things. It's the Holy Spirit that gives us the insight, the power, courage, and wisdom to endure and discern the spirit of a person. **Vision Chasers, people will tell you to watch them dogs. But I say, watch them snakes.**

A lot of Vision Chasers have been snake bitten (hurt, talked about, deceived, robbed, lied on, overtaken in sin, afflicted financially, attacked, etc.) and have stopped chasing the vision, stopped trying to build spiritual fire for themselves and the people of God and just laid down to die. Just because you have been snake bitten, doesn't mean you have to lay down and die! You don't have to drop your torch and quit. You just have to shake it off and rest in God's grace. In **Acts 28:3**, Paul had gathered a bundle of sticks and laid them on the fire when a viper came out of the heat and fastened on his hand. Paul is gathering wood for a fire. He just came through a hard trial, a storm, and a shipwreck. The last few months of his life haven't been good. He has been before Felix and Agrippa and is still a prisoner. But he is trying to stir up a fire, trying to add fuel, to get warmed up again to chase the vision God has given him and a snake bites him. Notice the snake didn't bite anyone else. **The devil knows who to attack.**

Snakes are funny. **They lie dormant as long as it is cold.** They aren't even noticeable in cold environments; they just blend in with their surroundings. But just wait until the fire is started, wait until the Vision is moving forward, and things warm up. When things in ministry heat up, the business begins to prosper, your family begins to prosper--the snakes are going to show up!

Once, I was preaching a series of messages titled: "Break Every Chain" and the Holy Spirit really moved, several people received their healing and deliverance. The church was on fire! That following Monday I walked into the lobby of the church and there was a real live snake at the door. I killed the snake and kept moving forward in God. A year later we were expanding our outreach programs and community development projects, the community was truly being blessed. I was bringing food into the Multipurpose room of the church for our community food pantry, and I saw a snake in the flowerbed next to the entrance. I tried to kill it, but it got away. Several weeks later I was again in the multipurpose room working with our youth (our youth were on fire for God). I went into the bathroom and there was the same identical snake in the toilet. One of our teens (Boston) and I killed the snake with a pair of hedge clippers. **The more I chased the**

Vision the more snakes kept coming. The real snakes were just a sign that spiritual snakes were also in the church, and more were coming to try to destroy the fellowship and derail the fire of the vision. But God and His Holy Spirit was always protecting us and giving us discernment.

Before Paul could witness or minster, a viper used its mouth to try to fill him with poison. But Paul didn't swell up. He didn't swell up with anger or fear. He just shook it off into the fire because he was full of the anti-venom of the Holy Spirit. Paul had been bitten, and the people around him aren't talking to him. **They are talking about him.** They are not trying to help, and some have even written him off as dead. It's amazing how church people will hear that you are going through and instead of helping and encouraging you, they distance themselves and talk about you.

As a Vision Chaser you will encounter snakes trying to fill you with discouragement, depression, fear, and anger. Snakes will lie to you that saying they are hearing from God on your behalf, but it may all be part of their poison scheme to make your Vision their vision or their vision your vision. In those times, reflect on **Psalms 140:1-3.** David wrote: "Deliver me, O Lord from the violent man. (2) which imagine mischiefs in their heart; continually they are gathering together for war. (3) They have sharpened their tongues like a serpent; added poison under their lips." Also heed **Ecclesiastes 10:11** which compares a gossiper to a snake: "Surely the serpent will bite without enchantment, and a **babbler** is no better."

Vision Chaser, know that the venom of a snake bite is designed to kill you and your vision. Like Paul, people will be watching you to see how you react. How will you react in times of trial, in times of trouble, in the midst of a pandemic, lockdowns and quarantines? Will you swell up with hatred, envy, fear, bitterness, depression, or unbelief? Will you wallow in self-pity, or will you quit and die? Will you, like Paul, by the strength and power of the Holy Spirit, shake it off and keep moving forward?

Vision Chasers who are called to be Shepherds need to know that Sheep need protection from **Adders (Vipers) snakes.** Adder is a word derived from an Old English term meaning serpent. Adders are small brown venomous snakes that live underground. They come out of their holes to bite sheep. The small bite causes an infection and if not treated—the sheep will die. To prevent the adder from popping out of the hole the Shepherd anoints the hole with oil—making the hole slippery for the snake to climb out. One of the biblical functions of the Visionary Shepherd is to protect the flock. The Shepherd puts oil on the sheep's head that acts as a repellant, so if an Adder does manage to come near, the smell drives the serpent away. Because of this the sheep are able to graze in abundance right in the enemy's presence. In **Psalm 23** God is the Shepherd and we are His Sheep, so when **verse 5** says "he anoints my head with oil" David is reminding us of what a Shepherd does for the Sheep. The function of the CEO or President of a company is to protect the employees and stability of the business. The function of the Head of Household is to protect the family at every level especially spiritually, physically, and financially.

As a Vision Chaser you must know that all fiery serpents are not sent from the enemy, some are sent from God because of disbelief and disobedience. In **Numbers 21:1-9** the people of Israel are on the brink of victory. They are about to start defeating the nation of Canaan after spending 40 years wandering around the wilderness. They are about to enter the Promised Land that God had promised them. They are one step from victory when the Bible has these tragic words to say. "The people become impatient **(tired of waiting)** because of the journey." **(Numbers 21:4)**

Here is what impatience is: it is taking your eyes off God and putting them back on your circumstances. It is dismissing God, His ways, and His timing, and instead believing that you have a better way. Impatient is when you start to become distrustful of God, and His plan, and you start to become dissatisfied with the provisions of God. I have seen this time and time again in ministry, family decisions and business. Somebody is running well, going on with God, growing and enjoying the richness of grace-and they start to become impatient, weary, and resentful. They start to second guess, get defiant, start to wave a fist at God and become critical. And that is exactly what Israel did. They got tired of the manna. Vision Chasers we must trust the process of God and not become impatient. **Numbers 21:4-9** states: They traveled from Mount Hor along the route to the Red Sea, to go around Edom. But the people grew impatient on the way; they spoke against God and against Moses, and said, "Why have you brought us up out of Egypt to die in the desert? There is no bread! There is no water! And we detest this miserable food!" Then the Lord sent venomous snakes among them. They bit the people and many Israelites died. The people came to Moses and said, "We sinned when we spoke against the Lord and against you. Pray that the Lord will take the snakes away from us." So, Moses prayed for the people. The Lord said to Moses, "Make a snake and put it up on a pole; anyone who is bitten can look at it and live." So, Moses made a bronze snake.

It is important to note that the Bible does not say that God takes the snakes away, He just provides a means by which the Israelites' lives can be saved. All of us have been bitten by the same snake and unless we have put our trust in the One who was lifted up, **we are dying and don't know it. John 3:14-15** says, "Just as Moses lifted up the snake in the desert, so the Son of Man must be lifted up, that everyone who believes in him may have eternal life. Vision Chasers know that the snakes are coming, but just look up to Jesus and He will give you-life and strength to stay in the race.

THE INSIDE MAN

When you accept your Vision from God, you will be attacked by outside snakes as well as demons who have attached themselves to you internally. Their purpose is to keep you from serving God effectively and pursuing your ministry, family, and business dreams as a Vision Chaser. As much as it is necessary for you to deal with the attacks from your surroundings, you must also deal with the demons that have connected themselves to you and seek to evict you from your own body and calling.

In 2006, there was a movie titled **"Inside Man",** an American crime thriller film directed by Spike Lee. It centers on an elaborate bank heist on Wall Street over a 24-hour period. The film stars Denzel Washington as Detective Keith Frazier, the NYPD's hostage negotiator, Clive Owens as Dalton Russell, the mastermind who orchestrates the heist, and Jodie Foster as Madeleine White, a Manhattan "power broker" who becomes involved when the bank's founder, Arthur Case (Christopher Plummer), asks her to keep something in his safe deposit box protected from the robbers. It is called the "Inside Man" because Clive Owens hides behind a fake wall inside the bank he has robbed until people have stopped searching for him. A full week after the robbery, he walks out of the bank, passes right by Denzel Washington, and slips a diamond inside of Denzel's pocket with a note about the safe deposit box. The movie is intriguing because no one ever finds out who the inside man really is. He makes all of these external demands to officers and demands of the hostages, without ever revealing his true identity. If you are to move forward chasing the vision, you must ask and answer the question: **Is there something on the inside of me that is hindering my pursuit of the vision that needs to come out?** Is there something on the inside of you that is so well hidden that you have even forgotten that it is there? Is there something **inside of you** that you have locked away and don't want anyone else to find? Is there some evil spirit deep down on the **inside of you** that is really calling the shots in your life? Has that something on the **inside of you** consumed you until the real you is almost lost?

In **Mark 5:1-6** scriptures states, *"They went across the lake to the region of the Gerasenes. When Jesus got out of the boat, a man with an impure spirit came from the tombs to meet him. This man lived in the tombs, and no one could bind him anymore, not even with a chain. For he had often been chained hand and foot, but he tore the chains apart and broke the irons on his feet. No one was strong enough to subdue him. Night and day among the tombs and in the hills, he would cry out and cut himself with stones. When he saw Jesus from a distance, he ran and fell on his knees in front of him."* In the gospel of Luke, it says, this man was naked. Thus, he is a naked man, living in a cemetery, cutting himself with stones. Crying out all day and all night. Everyone considered him to be crazy, but it was really the result of something that was on the inside of him. He was outcast and misunderstood. They shunned and scorned him. They called him a mad man and treated him like a freak show. He was hopeless and helpless until Jesus set him free!

Have you ever had something on the inside of you that didn't belong? There was a man named Lawrence who lived in Thousand

Oaks, California who came home from work to discover that his roof and his chimney had been dismantled. He discovered that the authorities had dismantled his house to pull a woman out of his chimney who had gotten stuck 8 feet down the chimney. Apparently, the woman who had gotten stuck in the chimney, was someone he had met online, as a result of online dating. He had gone on a couple of dates with her and made up in his mind that she was not the one. So, the young woman wanted to give Lawrence a piece of her mind. She showed up to the house. She knocked on the door and got no response from Lawrence because he was not home. She was determined for the two of them to have a face-to-face conversation. The door was locked, so she tried the windows. The windows were locked. In her mind, the only logical thing to do was to climb on the roof and go down the chimney. She got stuck halfway down and began to scream for help. The next-door neighbors heard the screaming and called 911. The fire department come and without success was unable to pull the woman out. So, they decided to dismantle the chimney and the roof in an attempt to pull the woman out. Lawrence come home from work and discovered that the outside of his house was messed up and destroyed, because there was something on the inside that didn't belong.

The man living in the graveyard was just like the house of Lawrence. They both had something on the inside that didn't belong. Before you can be successful chasing the vision whatever is on the inside of you that would hinder you—has to be removed.

Just because you have been called to serve as a Visionary, an Ambassador, or a Future Torch Bearer, does not mean you are immune from internal spiritual attack. Just because you have a family plan and budget doesn't mean that the devil wont try to sabotage it. Most of us need to be spiritually dismantled like the roof of Lawrence's house so we can get to the root of our internal and external issues. Many of us are dealing with messy relationships, friendships, money management, visions, dreams, businesses, and ministries. The reason why things on the external are so messed up is because there are some things on the internal that are messed up. Many of us, have given Jesus our hand, but body, soul and spirit still need to be delivered from some stuff.

Deliverance is difficult because Satan has convinced us that nothing is wrong. The problem is our mind. So, as a man thinketh, so is he. The devil reaches us through our mind. We must take charge of what we think. *"For though we walk in the flesh, we do not war according to the flesh, for the weapons of our warfare are not of the flesh, but divinely powerful for the destruction of fortresses. We are destroying speculations and every lofty thing raised up against the knowledge of God, and we are taking every thought captive to the obedience of Christ* **(2 Corinthians 10:3-5). In order to be delivered from something, you must believe that there is something you need deliverance from, and that God can deliver you.**

Vision Chasers, the Bible lets us know that the man is dealing with an internal issue that he hasn't properly addressed. Because he has not properly addressed his internal issue it has manifested itself so much so until he is participating in self-destructive behavior. As we embark on this journey to become visionaries each of us must begin to search ourselves and see what it is internally that is causing us to act externally in an ungodly manner. What is inside of you that is causing you to participate in destructive behaviors? What is causing you to sin, drink, smoke, lie, take drugs, commit adultery, engage in fornication, gossip, attempt suicide, participate in unethical business practices, etc.? What is inside your closet? Your skeleton room. The one you hide from and lie about. Most of the problems we face are because of the battles that goes on inside of us. Every conflict begins with us: in our body, our mind, in our emotions. The war rages inside us. **Romans 7:19—23** "For what I do is not the good I want to do, no, the evil I do not want to do, this I keep on doing. Now if I do not want to do it, it is no longer I who do it, but it is sin living in me that I do it. So, I find this law at work, when I want to do good, evil is right there with me. For in my inner being I delight in God's law, but I see another law at work in the members of my body, waging war against the law of my mind and making me a prisoner of the law of sin at work within my members." There is a battle for your strengths, energy, dreams, and vision. Everyone has these battles in our minds. It is what we do with them that matters.

If you choose to ignore the internal issues you will find yourself connected with dead people, in dead places, in dark circumstances and the only reason will be- that there is something going on internally that you have not properly addressed through godly deliverance. Do not be misled: *"Bad company corrupts good character."* **(1 Corinthians 15:33 NIV).** Even the character of your ministry and business can be corrupted. Spanish novelist Miguel de Cervantes stated: "Tell me what company thou keepest, and I'll tell thee what thou art". **As with any journey, who you travel with can affect your destination.**

How do you know if you are connected to a dead person? Dead people are not going anywhere. Dead people are stagnated. Dead people are stuck. Dead people have no dreams and no vision. Dead people have no ambition, no goals. Dead people can't think or relate to life situations. It is vital to do a personal assessment of what is being manifested externally in your life **(your inside man).** I tell you the same thing my mother used to tell me when I was a kid, "you need to check yourself before you wreck yourself."

The Bible says the man is living in the graveyard. **Graveyards are full of lost potential. Plans that were never developed. Inventions that were never designed. Dreams that never came to pass. Songs that were never written or sung. Books that were never written. Paintings that never made it to the canvass. Businesses that were never opened. Ideas that were never shared and visions that never became a reality.** He was dead without faith, a future, or family. He had no shelter, no dignity, sensitivity, or shame. He is naked and actively participating in self-destructive behavior. He was dealing with all of these problems, issues, and circumstances and his solution is chains and shackles. It's a solution, but it's the wrong solution. Just because you made a decision doesn't mean it was the right one. **He comes up with an external solution for an internal problem.**

He is using the wrong solution because he has not properly diagnosed the root of his problem. The Bible lets us know the man, even in the midst of his hell, in the midst of his issues, trials and tribulations—sees Jesus at a distance. **(Mark 5:6).** Vision Chasers don't allow your issues to blind you to the point where you cannot see Jesus. Don't allow your depression to distract you from the Savior. Don't allow the stress of this pandemic to distract you from the deliverer. Always look to see Jesus at a distance.

The Bible says not only did the man see Jesus in the midst of his hell and chaos, but Jesus also saw him. The first thing Jesus wants to do when He sees you is to address your identity. Jesus knows your past, present and future. He knows that you have been dealing with some dead people in a dead place. You have subjected yourself to self-destructive behavior. You have been dealing with a lot of internal issues, pressures, stress, anxiety that has gone unchecked. Yet He still wants to know how do you identify yourself? Have you forgotten who you are and whose you are? Have you forgotten that you are a Vision Chaser: **Visionary, Ambassador and Future Torch Bearer?**

Your identity is the starting point for all actions and decisions you make. How you view yourself influences your world view. That's why it is important that as a Vision Chaser, you know who you are in Christ. **Proverbs 23:7** states: "As a man thinketh in his heart, so is he." So, if you think you are broken, you are going to relate to people as if you are broken. If you think you are substandard or beneath other people—that's how you will live your life. But if you think and believe that God is able to heal, deliver and restore. If you believe that He is a rewarder to them who diligently seek him—then despite what you are facing – you will walk in the power of His might.

Jesus said, what's your name? Because I need to address your nature before I can direct you to your purpose. Notice that it wasn't the man who responded, but the inside man, (**one of the demons responded**) and said, "We are Legion". The demon was letting Jesus know that we have taken control of his body and mind so much so until the man is incapable of speaking for himself. Jesus asked the question, because He needed the man to know that before I can prepare you for your future, I need to separate you from the things that are dead in your life. Jesus spoke to the demon and the demon came out of the man and the man was delivered. Jesus through His holy word is always speaking to us to remind us of who we are in Him. The Bible **(the Word)** says you are fearfully and wonderfully made. You are made in the image of God. You are a "Vision Chaser".

Nothing sets the atmosphere for deliverance like the Word of God. That's why there is such an attack on Vision Chasers. **What the enemy sends after you-is proof that he knows what's in you.** That's why there is such an attack on the Preacher, Families and Christian Businesses, because there is an attack on the WORD. Because the devil knows if he can stop people from hearing the Word, he can slow down their pursuit for Jesus and divine deliverance. The Spirit World only responds to the **WORD**! You can't sing a demon away. You can't shout a demon away. **Deliverance takes the WORD!** Man shall not live by bread alone, but by every **WORD** that preceded out of the mouth of God. Whatever role you are called to play as a Vision Chaser, you are going to need the **WORD**.

Jesus called the demons out and allowed the demons to enter into the swine or pigs and drove them off a cliff into the river where they drowned. **The man got delivered but deliverance like vision - comes at price.** The Bible says the Jewish community got upset with Jesus to the point that they tried to run Jesus out of town. They didn't eat pigs because of their dietary customs, but they sold them, they made money off of them. They wanted the man delivered, but they didn't want it to cost them anything. People want success but don't want to pay the cost. Most people that need deliverance won't get delivered, because of what it might cost them. People will stop chasing the vision, because of what it costs them. Families don't stick to a budget because of the sacrifices they will have to make to maintain it. What price are you willing to pay for your deliverance and destiny? Maybe you decided to be like the bank's founder in "Inside Man", Arthur Case (Christopher Plummer), who was more willing to pay the price to keep something in his safe deposit box than allow it to be released, thus freeing himself from his past.

Now, at the end of the story, the man who was naked has clothes on and he is in his right mind. The man who was once in a dead place, with dead people is now sitting at the feet of Jesus. The man asked Jesus if he could go with him. But Jesus said in **Mark 5:19-20:** "go home to thy friends and tell them what great things the Lord hath done for thee, and hath had compassion on thee. And he departed, **as a Vision Chaser in ministry of Jesus Christ, and as an Ambassador** and began to publish in Decapolis the great things Jesus had done for him: and all men did marvel." Jesus is still able to deliver. He can deliver you into your destiny. **Be transformed FROM THE INSIDE –OUT into a "Vision Chaser" for the kingdom.**

PROBLEMS, PROBLEMS, PROBLEMS

Life is a series of problem-solving opportunities. The problems you face will either defeat you or define and develop you depending on how you handle them. **2 Corinthians 4:8-12** says. We are hard pressed on every side, but not crushed, perplexed, but not in despair, persecuted but not abandoned; struck down, but not destroyed... One of the things we should realize is, even though we are faithful Christians and Vision Chasers problems will come and battles will have to be fought. Vision Chasers like everyone else are constantly facing one problem after another such as bereavement, homelessness, joblessness, sickness, Covid-19, marital issues, immigration issues, financial problems, family problems, business failure, etc. Problem-solving is a universal job skill that we must all recognize and address.

A problem is never a problem until the person who has the problem perceives it to be a problem. A problem is defined as a matter or situation regarded as unwelcomed or harmful and needing to be dealt with and overcome. A problem is denoting or relating to people whose behavior causes difficulties to themselves and others. A problem is something that is the source of trouble, worry, etc. A problem is any question or matter involving doubt, uncertainty, or difficulty. The Covid-19 pandemic is a problem and change does not happen until the person with the problem wants to do something about it. When America realized we had a pandemic-we shut down and went into quarantine. Our government mandated everyone to wear a mask, and gloves, use sanitizer, and practice social distancing. Our government has not just looked at the aftereffects of the coronavirus, but the internal affects as well. How do we stop it? Is the vaccine the solution to the problem?

As Visionaries, Ambassadors and Future Torch Bearers we must constantly search ourselves for internal problems and address them appropriately. Whenever you only use external solutions for an internal problem all you really do is perpetuate the problem on the inside. When a problem goes unaddressed, the problem gets worse.

We may not live in the cemetery as the man in the previous chapter, but there are some Visionaries who are spiritually dead… and only Jesus Christ can revive and set free! We can't keep trying to cover up the problem with a nice hello and a smile. Covering the problem with clothes, money, houses, and cars. You are like Hospice **(treating for comfort and calling it success because you are trying to ease the pain.)** We have convinced ourselves that as long as we are successful in the eyes of the world, we don't have a problem. **However, our biggest problem is not failure in business. Our biggest problem is succeeding at the wrong thing. For what does it profit a man to gain the whole world and still lose his soul.** Outward success becomes a narcotic if not properly addressed. The devil wants to destroy you…Jesus wants to deliver you! But we must get to the root of the problem. As Visionaries we must deal with problems. When you are spending more money than you make—that's a problem. When you are a Christian business, and you are not implementing Christian principals—that's a problem.

As individuals we all have problems. As a country all we have to do is turn on the news and see—we got problems. We all have our own pandemic tragedy. How do we stop a potential pandemic from spreading? In order to properly address the catastrophic impact of the pandemic on the U.S. economy and external consequences such as the spread of the infectious disease through global travel and trade, we have to accurately identify the cause of the illness. We have to train ourselves to track and contain outbreaks by using an effective emergency management system. We have to find a cure not just a vaccine. We must solve the problem.

Every business at some level has problems. But as Vision Chasers, we must be able to see Jesus at a distance. **Vision is all about seeing at a distance.** The ultimate solution for your problems chasing the vision is about being able to go back and look at the written Vision, Mission statement, Household or Business Plan and remembering why you started this journey in the first place. You may be having business problems, ministry problems, relationship problems, financial problems, family issues, health issues, but I encourage you to stay focused on the vision that God had you to put in writing. **Don't allow your problem to keep you from the problem solver.**

Problem solving is Biblical. Problem solving is working through the details systematically by considering all sides of an issue. It's an acquired skill.

1. **Identify the problem**
2. **Determine what caused the problem**
3. **Figure out different ways to solve the problem**
4. **Pray and seek God's guidance about the problem**

5. **Search the scripture to see how related problems were solved**
6. **Ask for God's wisdom**
7. **Follow God's lead and direction and implement the best possible solution to the problem.**

Problem solving when applied properly to business contributes to business prosperity. When properly applied to Ministry- the ministry becomes stronger. When properly applied to family relationships become unbreakable. Don't allow the breakdowns in your life to keep you from Christ and the faith. **Just because you are saved, you can't put life in park.** Keep your eyes on Jesus—God will give you the strength to continue chasing after Him and His will.

SILENCING THE NOISE

Dear Lord, in a world of distractions, help me to focus on you. This is my prayer because I know **if the devil can't destroy you, he will try to distract you.** Sometimes what cripples us – are not demons, but too much noise in our heads. My childhood Pastor (Rev. C.D. Tate) would always say: **"Don't allow the giants to be louder than the grapes."** It's a loud noisy world we live in and the Covid-19 pandemic, Black Lives Matter, All Lives Matter, Defunding the Police, Racism, our Political and economic landscape, etc. has only made it worst. On top of all this Satan the accuser of the brothers is still speaking falsely about the believer. He is the inventor of **Weapons of Mass Distraction.** He is always trying to manipulate believers to question and doubt the validity of their relationship with God. He spends his time pointing out past failures and enticing us to new ones. He tries to hide the fact that if you have repented that God has already forgiven you of your sins because Jesus died for sinners like you. Every time you attempt to move forward in pursuit of your divine destiny, Satanic critics shows up to parade your dirty laundry. Satan handcuffs your spirit by always having an accuser in your midst—whose sole purpose is to remind you that your past will never be behind you. **They** have convinced themselves that your past justifies their present actions. But if you are going to "Chase the Vision", you are going to have to learn to silence the noise of the enemy. **The noise is an attempt by demonic forces to separate you from your possibilities.** The noise is the voice of the dream killers who don't think you should be in business for yourself or that your family deserves to prosper. Our minds can easily be led astray from obedience to God if we allow our thoughts to be deceived by the enemy.

In order to move forward as a Visionary, an Ambassador or Future Torch Bearer you have to learn how to silence the noise. How do you silence the attacks, threats, doubts, confusion, lies, fake news, and accusations of haters? The first thing you must know is that anything the devil says, the opposite is true. He is a liar. Secondly, you must learn spiritual warfare. Spiritual warfare is taking a stand against preternatural evil forces. It is recognizing that evil spirits are able to intervene in human affairs. As Vision Chasers, you must battle against such evil spirits with the power of God, Jesus Christ, and the Holy Spirit. "For we wrestle not against flesh and blood, but against principalities, against powers, against the rulers of the darkness of this world, against spiritual wickedness in high places." ***Ephesians 6:12.*** The devil works through people that look just like you and me. He is a puppet master, and people are his puppets. **We must not lose sight of who is behind our destruction.** We are at war, not with terrorist, not with mankind, but with the devil. We must discern the snakes and silence the noise. In order to stop the noise created by the devil (the lies, attacks, threats, and accusations, undermining and condescending attitudes) you must understand how to use spiritual warfare. In times past, noise didn't last long and couldn't travel very far. But today technology allows us to take our voices to the end of the earth. A YouTube video can go viral in a day and make the 7pm news. Reaching the world no longer takes much money or great ability. All it takes is an internet connection. All of this has given Satan easier access to your mind.

However, the same tools that Satan will try to use to spread lies, Vision Chasers should be using the same technology and social media platforms to spread truth, including Facebook, Instagram, Twitter, and Church websites. Among young Americans: nearly 90 percent of young adults ages 18 to 29, are using social media. Social media transcends geography, connects family and friends across the globe. Information once relegated to encyclopedias and Sunday morning bulletins, is now at our fingertips. And meaningful messages, including the message of the gospel of Jesus Christ are shared with ease. The devil knows you are chasing the Vision God gave you. This has placed a bull's eye on your back and placed you in the crosshairs of his scope. You are now in a Spiritual battle for your destiny. So, it is important that you understand the art of war, to ensure victory. Know that Satan's intentions are not to delay your destiny, but to destroy it—by destroying you. Paul stated in **2 Timothy 3:6** "that we would be overwhelmed by sin and swayed by all kinds of desires." Satan and his minions desire to overwhelm you with noise and distractions. Overwhelmed means to be so bombarded by something until it defeats you. The whole purpose of Sin is to destroy. The bible says the wages of sin is death. But the gift of God is eternal life.

The word "But" is a transition—which means it connects what succeeds it with what preceded it. Life is full of BUTS. A BUT is that frustrating, painful, sometimes embarrassing moment of our lives—that we really can't do anything about except own it. It is that something that is so big that only God can change. It's the illness that the doctors can't fix. It's the condition you have to live with the rest of your life. It's the addiction you can't seem to shake. It's the dark secret that you don't want to get exposed. It's the sin that you committed that still has consequences. Whenever you see BUT—there is going to be a transitional phrase right after it. So, if things have been bad on the front, it's going to be better after BUT. **That means the worst has already passed—and the best is yet to come.** This is the kingdom mindset of a "Vision Chaser". That's why you don't quit—you can take a break, get a second wind for the second mile—because BUT is about to happen. That's why you don't turn to drugs, alcohol, porn, infidelity, or any other sin to fill the void, BUT is about to take place. In ministry—your best days are ahead of you. In your marriage—your best days are ahead. In your family and finances—your best days are ahead. In Business the best days are ahead. When you consider all the hell you have gone through since this pandemic—God is pushing your BUT. So, hold on, help is on the way.

Satan's job is to see to your failure and decline. He knows that in order to be successful, he must control your mind and thinking. He intentionally sets us up to be consumed by our fleshly desires. That's right, it's a setup, a scheme, a trick intended to incriminate you by overwhelming you with sin leaving you covered in guilt and shame—and then he hits you with the accusation: **and you're supposed to be a Christian.** You're supposed to be a leader in the Kingdom of God. You're supposed to be a Christian Business. The accusation by the enemy is so loud because the intent is to silence your voice. His intent is to stop you dead in your tracks. His intent is to have you quit, to walk away. But I'm here to tell you—rest if you must, but don't you quit. **The only thing quitting accomplishes is guarantee that the vision will never happen.** Regroup and refocus if you must, but don't you quit. Don't you check out just yet, don't you cry Susie-yet. I know you have some regrettable experiences and some of your sinful actions have caused some guilt and shame. But you still have a divine calling on your life. You still have a divine purpose. You still have a Holy Ghost anointing that will be even stronger as you continue to Chase the Vision.

It's time for spiritual warfare. Time to get deliverance from the satanic voices and noise. Everything that has happened in your life has a divine purpose. There is no such thing as chance or happenstance. You are not a creature of a moment; you are a Child of God. You are not directed by events; you are called to direct events. God did not give the day to destroy you but gave you the day to make things happen. He made you the head and not the tail. You are up and not down. You are a lender and not a borrower, because this is the blessing of the Sons and Daughters of Abraham. This is your inheritance, and it starts by understanding that the things you are going through are happening for a reason. So, I warn you to stay alert. "Stay alert (knowing) your enemy the devil prowls like a roaring lion, looking for someone to devour." **(1 Peter 5:8).** Remember what's behind you no longer defines you. You should not give your past room to roam free in your head. You must silence the noise. The Bible says in **Numbers 3:30** that Caleb silenced the crowd. He said, shut up! We've heard enough of your negativity. Sometimes you got to cancel out the noise that is in your ear. You got to stop talking to negative people. **You can't hang out with negative people and expect to live a positive life.** You've got to block phone numbers, text messages and take a break from social media. **You've got to engage in noise cancelation.**

It was Wednesday, August 22, 2018, I was at the Beacon Riverfront park sitting trying to meditate on God's word and listen to some gospel music. As I sat there on the bench the guys working for the Beacon Recreation Department came and said they were about to start cutting the grass, but I was not in their way. So, I sat there and continued to listen to my music trying to concentrate on the things of God, when all of a sudden, the lawn mowers started running and I could barely hear my music. Then the train started on the railroad tracks behind me. The noise was so loud I was about to give up listening to my music until one of the young men went into his truck and said you can use these while we continue to cut the grass. He said these are made by Bose, they are **noise cancelation** headphones.

When there is a lot of noise around you—**get you some spiritual noise cancelation headphones of faith.** Start listening to gospel music, declaring favor, and rebuking the enemy, reading your Word, and praying in the Spirit. Listen to a recording of one of your Pastor's messages, or some motivational recordings on how to take your business to the next level. When life gets noisy, that's not the time to give up and quit. When things get hard, that's the time to cancel out the negativity by going to God in prayer. Caleb tells the crowd to be quiet. Then he declares that despite the negativity of the ten (10) our God is more than able to give us the victory. God promised us this land. We have a divine reservation for promise—all we have to do is trust God and follow His direction. Chasing the Vision is a great undertaking; making Noise cancelation very necessary if you intend to continue. The noise is going to come from everywhere. The noise is coming to destroy you by distracting you. Because the devil is trying to control the narrative of your destiny. But you must decide that your confidence in God and the Vision will not be shaken.

GOING THE EXTRA MILE

You are a Visionary, an Ambassador or Future Torch Bearer called by God to Chase the Vision in ministry and business for the benefit and welfare of your family. You have learned who you are and why you have been called. You are utilizing the power of the Holy Spirit to discern snakes and how to look to God to survive after being bitten. You have addressed the inside man and silenced the noise so you could stay focus on reaching your goal of running the race that is set before you. **But you must go the extra mile.** The term "going the extra mile" is an old expression. It describes individuals that always do a little more than what's expected. In Business we go the extra mile for our clients or customers. Without their clients' businesses wouldn't exit. In family we go the extra mile by putting family first. In Ministry we go the extra mile so that God will get the honor and glory from our actions and behavior.

It was **7 PM October 20th, 1968.** The crowd is about to leave the Olympic Stadium in Mexico City. The last of the runners were being carried off in stretchers. When all of a sudden, the crowd stopped. There was a flurry of activity as one lone runner from Tanzania, number 36 came limping into the stadium far behind the rest. He had fallen and injured his leg. He hobbled with each bloody step. They asked him at the finish line, "Why did you finish the race when you were so badly injured? He said, "My country didn't send me 7,000 miles to start the race. They sent me 7,000 miles to finish the race. He was an Ambassador and Torch Bearer of light for his country, and he refuse to drop his flame.

Vision Chasers, are you ready to go the extra mile? Are you determined to finish the race? **Matthew 5:41** states: "And whosoever shall compel thee to go a mile, go with him twain." The call to go the second mile was not a popular call for the Jews. It was an inconvenient demand, often associated with a reluctant and complaining spirit. I am reminded of a story about a young teenage boy that had just gotten his driver's license. When he got home, he asked his father, who was a minister, if they could discuss the use of the car. His father took him into his study and said to the boy, "I'll make a deal with you. If you bring up your grades, study your Bible a little more, and get a haircut, then we'll talk about the use of the car."

After about a month, the boy came back and again asked his father if they could discuss the use of the car. They again went to the father's study where his father said, "Son, I've been so very proud of you. You have brought up your grades, you've studied your Bible diligently, but you didn't get your haircut." The young man waited a moment and replied, "Dad, I've been thinking about that. You know, Samson had long hair, Moses had long hair, Noah had long hair, even Jesus had long hair..." His father interrupted him at that point and said, "Yes son, and they walked everywhere they went!"

He was so close, yet so far, from getting what he wanted. The boy was willing to pay most of the price, but not all of the price. The boy knew what he wanted. His desire was strong. But there was a problem: he wasn't willing to go all the way. He wasn't willing to pay the entire price. Vision Chasers are you willing to pay the price for victory and success?

Unfortunately, most of us are only willing to go so far with God, our vision, business, career, family financial stability, etc. We are willing to go only so far with the church and the call on our life. When your boss ask you perform a different role, you are quick to say that is not in my job description. When we get to that point, we stop. We find ourselves backing up, pulling away, or being unwilling to get any closer to God or to our church family and we stop the chase. In business we chose profit over Christian values and principals. But Jesus commands us to go the distance.

The command of Jesus given in **Matthew 5:41** comes as an exhortation that such a call should not be performed by a sullen, wilted spirit. In every life there are unwelcome circumstances that will force themselves upon the saint of God. There will be injustices, there will be omissions of recognition, there will be hurts along the way, there will be tasks that have to be taken merely out of necessity and not of choice (like being the CEO and Administrative Assistant at the same time). On the whole, this world has a one-mile concept. Do just enough to get by. But those who are willing to go the second mile, place themselves in a category of two-milers.

Sadly enough, the one-mile concept affects the Church and Vision Chasers also. Lives are sterile of the power of God because there is just enough prayer to get by. Just enough church attendance to get by. Give just enough time and just enough of our finances to squeak through a relationship with God. We work our business plan just enough to employ ourselves instead of working toward expansion to employ others. We must be willing to go the extra mile. Like personalization and exceeding customer expectations. Referring to people by name whenever possible. Never forgetting what you promised and deliver on what you promised.

Vision Chasers more is required of us. The Psalmist, **Johnson Oatman, Jr.** illustrates best what would happen to those few who were willing to go the extra-mile that Jesus encouraged.

1. **If I walk in the pathway of duty,**
If I work till the close of the day,
I shall see the great King in His beauty,
When I've gone the last mile of the way.

   o **Refrain:**
   When I've gone the last mile of the way,
   I will rest at the close of the day;
   And I know there are joys that await me,
   When I've gone the last mile of the way.

2. **If for Christ I proclaim the glad story,**
If I seek for His sheep gone astray,
I am sure He will show me His glory,
When I've gone the last mile of the way.

3. **Here the dearest of ties we must sever,**
Tears of sorrow are seen every day;
But no sickness, no sighing forever,
When I've gone the last mile of the way.

And if here I have earnestly striven,
And have tried all His will to obey,
Twill enhance all the rapture of heaven,
When I've gone the last mile of the way.

Sometimes even the best of us fall when life overwhelms us, or sin overtakes us. When the difficulties of life come, when you fall in the race, the choice is yours: You can stay down and out, or you can get to your feet and strive for the second mile. If God has called you to "Chase the Vision", then you got to be a two miler.

If we "Chase the Vision" we must accept those things in life that cannot be changed (like our past). **Isaiah 43:18-19** says, "Forget the former things, do not dwell on the past. See, I am doing a new thing!" We must forget the past, even when those closest to us—do not. We must possess the ability to endure tough times. A person chasing the Vision must have a high level of what William Barclay described endurance as: **"the courageous acceptance of everything life can do to us and the transmitting of even the worst event into another step on the upward way."** Remember God is in charge of our lives. His desire is for us to grow in the likeness of His Son. We must learn and practice patience in order to grow. We do this by abiding with a God who is faithful. Success or failure may finally be determined by one's attitude toward opposition. **Ministries and businesses don't grow by accident. They do so by intentional design and planning.** Thus, we must pray to God for a spiritual second wind—to run the second mile and keep growing and moving forward.

Chasing the Vision is bigger than you. It is a relentless pursuit for something that won't rot, rust, corrode, be spent, or sold. You must not be narrow minded in the execution and implementation of your vision. You must encompass the larger concept of building a Christian business, raising a Christian family, and growing God's Kingdom. Chasing the Vision means you can't settle for less than greatness. Our society has become far too easily pleased. We've become intoxicated by what the world has to offer, and we have failed to sell out to something far bigger than what we are. So, I say to you—Chasing the Vision means giving your best action and attitude for Jesus, not just sometimes, but every time. Doesn't He deserve it? He gave us His all. How can we give Him less than our all? Chasing the Vision means taking ownership of your dreams, business plan, mission statement, family budget. Chasing the Vision for a believer means living what you say you believe. Vision Chasers don't quit when it gets tough. They don't go off whining and crying because things didn't go their way, or they got their feelings hurt. Chasing the Vision is taking ownership of the ministry or business you have been called to serve or operate. Chasing the Vision is never a losing effort. Vision Chasers never settle for second place, second best or for anything less than God.

We must continue relentlessly to move forward with the Vision. **We cannot rest on past victories or be paralyzed by past defeats.** We've got to get busy doing whatever God wants us to do to advance the gospel. To take your idea, dream, vision, business to the next level we must become Visionaries, Ambassadors and Torch Bearers. We don't have a moment to waste. You cannot become content. Mediocrity and complacency cannot be characteristics of a Vision Chaser. You can't just be around the church; you must be involved in the Church. You cannot just be an employee where you work, you must be an Ambassador. You can't just own a business, but it must be a business that practices Christian principals. You can't be near God's will; you must be in God's will. You can't just imagine your purpose; you must discover and fulfill your purpose. You can't just aim, but you must achieve. **2 Corinthians 7:21** states: "our purpose is to do what is right, not only in the sight of the Lord, but also in the sight of others." We must move forward. We must keep chasing the vision. If God is for us, who can stand against us. The same God who fought for

Israel—enables us to face all that comes our way. As long as we stay in the race and keep "Chasing the Vision", we will be "more than conquerors." **(Romans 8:37)**

You must become a two-miler. Because two-mile men and women make the devil mad. Two-mile men and women give demons migraines. Two-mile men and women grow in some of the most adverse conditions. The pits, the accusations, and the prisons that Joseph came out of seemed only to heighten his commitment, ambition, and his abilities. Stop complaining and remember what God had promised. Never once in the account in Genesis, will you find Joseph complaining about his lot in life. That was because he had never forgotten what God had promised. **Proverbs 3:5-6** "Trust in the LORD with all thine heart; and lean not unto thine own understanding." "In all thy ways acknowledge him, and he shall direct thy paths."

GROWING UP IN CHRIST

If the devil can't steal your identity, he will certainly try to stunt your growth. Covid-19 pandemic has tested ministries, companies, and families of all sizes to adjust their standard operating practices. Covid-19 has disrupted the business of the world and forced billons of people to step outside of their normal routines. Nevertheless, despite the pressure to give up and quit—we must adapt, overcome, and grow. Before you can ever get to your promise, you must first learn how to grow up and manage your pain. The more you chase the vision; the more God expects you to grow in your faith and knowledge of who He is. God does not expect you to stay a child. God does not expect your business to stay small. He doesn't expect your family not to grow and prosper. God desires for you to grow up in Him. **Always dream big in Christ—you will grow into it.** So, how do you grow in Christ, grow a Vision, a ministry, a business, a career in a Post Pandemic world? The pandemic has caused us all to develop new habits, new interest, and new ways to simply be relevant. So, the question becomes what's next? Once the world adjust and returns to a new normal—how shall the Vision grow?

While we all grow up physically, many of us fail, to some extent, to experience growth of our minds, wills, and emotions. **Most businesses and churches die simply because they don't develop a strategy for growth.** Just because your business starts out as a **"Mom and Pop"** store front, doesn't mean it has to stay that way. If it is your current opinion to never grow, take a hard look around. You've gotten comfortable and stopped having Vision. We all have room to grow spiritually, yet many of us have that growth arrested at a very early age, or, tragically, it never even began. As a Pastor, I have encountered a lot of people who have refused to grow up in some much-needed areas. Usually, the one that needs to grow up the most, is the one who is quick to point out how grown and mature they are. They are quick to tell you how long they have been in the church and how long they have been saved. Yet when it comes to dealing with certain issues you see just how immature and childish, they can be.

The call of a Visionary, Ambassador or Torch Bearer is one that requires maturity. One of the signs of maturity is the ability to walk away from people, places and things that are not supportive of your growth. Many of you, have found yourselves in the cross hairs of the devil because of the ungodly relationships you have developed. These ungodly relationships are toxic and toxicity stunts growth. Think about it? There is no growth in the relationship or for you internally because, like a newborn baby, you're waiting on someone else to change you. It is time for you to take your rightful place as a 2022 Visionary. Yesterday is over. Sad as it may seem. But change is the essence of life. When you grow up in Christ, even your thinking has to change. Paul declares in **1 Corinthians 13:11:** *"When I was a child, I spoke as a child, I understood as a child, I thought as a child: but when I became a man, I put away childish things."* This is why God desires for you to grow up in Him.

If you are going to be successful, you got to grow up. Instead of being traditional you have to be revelational. We are entering a **NEW ERA** and you have got to grow up. You have got to know who you are and start walking in your promise. **If you don't, you will find it difficult to accept that you are worthy enough, righteous enough, or powerful enough to bring the vision to fulfillment.** Further, *"You are a chosen race, a royal priesthood, a holy nation, a people belonging to God, that you may declare the praises of him who called you out of darkness into his wonderful light. Once you were not a people, but now you are the people of God; once you had not received mercy, but now you have received mercy."* **(I Peter 2:9-10)** It' time to grow up and be the person God has created and called you to be.

In order to mature in God, you must mature in the faith. There are certain opportunities, miracles, blessings, and wonders you can't see until you mature. There are certain privileges you can't enjoy until you mature and reach for it. You must have a real, living, thriving, and stable relationship with God by continuing to grow. A champion doesn't wait until he gets in a fight to start training for the fight. People who get to the championship have to train and go through a lot of other fights before they get to the big one. Similarly, God will take you through some fights, test, troubles, trials, and setbacks to prepare you for the big fights of your life. Goliath was not David's destiny. He was just a warmup for his destiny. **Your Goliath was not sent to kill you. It was sent to mature you.**

When you grow up in Christ, you can move from speaking by opinion to speaking with power and authority. The one who grows in Christ develops a relationship with Christ that is blatantly apparent to believers and unbelievers alike. **Acts 4: 13-14** informs us *'When they saw the courage of Peter and John and realized that they were unschooled ordinary men; they were astonished and took* *note that these men had been with Jesus.'* This scripture lets us know that relationship cannot be taught, bought, or sold, it must be experienced. This relationship is based on a deep and thorough conviction of the truth found in following the way of Christ. Further, because of this relationship, the Holy Spirit of God emboldens us to **speak with power and authority** and allows us to show the world who we are by calling on the name of Jesus. **Vision Chasers, you are nothing, if you cannot proclaim His name.** The destiny of your vision is connected to your Christian identity. Therefore, your identity is grounded in God whose identity is never shaken or altered. Are you a Visionary, an Ambassador, or a Torch Bearer? What name do you proclaim as you chase the vision?

The vision for your Church, your Business, your Organization, your Family all needs to grow like Bermuda grass. Down south, the kind of grass you want to plant in your yard is Bermuda grass because Bermuda grass grows in all types of weather. Bermuda grass will stay green all year. Bermuda grass grows even in a drought. Having a Bermuda grass attitude is saying, I don't care how bad the weather might be, we might be in the midst of a pandemic, but I'm going to grow anyhow. It doesn't matter that the business is having a bad year, I am not about to abandon ship. If, you are "Chasing the Vision", you need to have some Bermuda grass faith. You may be experiencing a drought in your life— but keep growing. Your business might be slow but be resilient. Continue to be who God has called you to be. You cannot expect to be perfected, established, elevated or enlarged---unless you are spiritually and mentally mature. The question is not can God do it; but can you handle it? Can you endure? Will you position yourself for growth?

"But you [Timothy], keep your head in all situations endure hardship, do the work of an evangelist, discharge all the duties of your ministry." **(2 Timothy 4:5).** Chasing the Vision is all about endurance. Endurance is defined as the power of going on despite difficulties. Popular colloquial phrases describe it as: "Keep on Keeping on," "Hang in there." "Don't Quit." Its synonyms are determination, perseverance, tenacity, stamina, and backbone. When endurance is used in the Bible it means "to abide under," to bear up courageously, "and to tarry or wait." Spiritual and mental maturity comes from trials. You have to learn how to wait when you don't want to; how to keep smiling even when you're crying on the inside; how to keep hoping when you've hurting; and how to keep going when you feel like quitting.

The Bible in **2 Timothy 2:3-4** states: "Thou therefore endure hardness, as a good soldier of Jesus Christ. No man that warred entangled himself with the affairs of this life; that he may please him who hath chosen him to be a soldier." **1 Corinthians 13:7 (NLT)** Love never gives up, never loses faith, is always hopeful, and endures through every circumstance. **Romans 5:3-5** states: "And not only that, but we also rejoice in our afflictions, because we know that afflictions produce endurance, endurance produces proven character, and proven character produces hope. This hope does not disappoint. To keep growing you must learn to endure. Apostle Paul understood endurance and suffering for the Lord Jesus. If you are going to be a Vision Chaser—you too will become familiar with endurance and suffering. Paul had been imprisoned, beaten, stoned, shipwrecked, hungry, homeless, cold, and destitute, but he never doubted God's presence in his life. He didn't quit, give up, regress, forget his identity, call, or vision.

Isaiah described a need for Vision Chasers to stay strong and keep soaring in their growth. "Do you not know? Have you not heard? Yahweh is the everlasting God, the Creator of the whole earth. He never grows faint or weary; there is no limit to His understanding. He gives strength to the weary and strengthens the powerless. Youths may faint and grow weary, and young men stumble and fall, but those who trust in the LORD will renew their strength; they will soar on wings like eagles; they will run and not grow weary; they will walk and not faint" **(Isaiah 40:28-31 NIV)**

The secret is found in affirming God's presence. The world says give up, drop out, run away. The pandemic has become a great excuse (explanation/justification) for quitting, but not for you. God says to just trust him, lean on him, and fall into his arms. He is with you to support and sustain you. He will give you hope, courage, and strength to continue. He has promised, "'My presence will go [with you], and I will give you rest'" **(Ex. 33:14)**. I've learned during my growing periods that to endure is more than just continuing to exist it is continuing to exist in the same manner as before the suffering began. You are not enduring (the pandemic)—if you throw your hands up in defeat. You can rest but you must keep Chasing the Vision. You must keep transforming, growing, and getting better.

Ignance Paderewski, Poland's famous concert pianist and prime minister, was giving a series of concerts. A mother, wishing to encourage her young son's progress at the piano, bought tickets for a performance. When the night arrived, they found their seats near the front of the concert hall and eyed the majestic Steinway waiting on stage. The mother spotted a friend in the audience and walked down the aisle to greet her. Seizing the opportunity to explore the wonders of the concert hall, the little boy eventually made his way through a door marked, "No Admittance." When the house lights dimmed, and the concert was about to begin, the mother returned to her seat and discovered that the child was missing.

Suddenly, the curtains parted, and spotlights focused on the impressive Steinway on stage. In horror, the mother saw her little boy sitting at the keyboard, innocently picking out, "Twinkle, Twinkle, Little Star." His mother gasped, but before she could retrieve her son, the great piano master appeared on the stage and quickly moved to the keyboard. He whispered to the boy, **"Don't quit - keep playing."** Leaning over, Paderewski reached down with his left hand and began filling in a bass part. Soon, his right arm reached around the other side, encircling the child, to add a running obbligato. Together, the old master and young novice held the crowd mesmerized.

In our quest for contagious character, unpolished and incomplete though we may be, it is the Master who surrounds us and whispers in our ear, time and again, **"Don't quit - keep playing."** And as we do, he augments and supplements until a work of amazing beauty is created. What we can accomplish on our own is hardly noteworthy. We try our best, but the results aren't exactly graceful flowing music. But with the hand of the Master, our character can truly be beautiful. Our responsibility is to not quit, to keeping playing; his part is to fashion a masterpiece. **Keep growing, don't quit.**

If you are "Chasing the Vision" you got to be strong enough to grow no matter what the conditions are. Because when you grow you are also becoming deeply rooted in Jesus Christ. There is a difference between superficial character and one that has clutched its roots deep around the Rock of Ages. There is something awe-inspiring about a man or woman who has everlasting strength and staunch character in the face of tribulation. Some men, in their relationship with God, find that time and eternity will not demoralize nor demolish them, but time will be their opportunity. Sometimes the pressures of life and business exist only to stretch you to find new opportunities. The pandemic of 2019 that still continues to this very day has yielded destruction for many, but opportunity to be victorious for those of us who have vision.

Are you close to quitting? Please don't do it. Let endurance prevail. "Blessed is a man who endures trials, because when he passes the test, he will receive the crown of life that He has promised to those who love Him" **(Jas. 1:12 NIV). Remember you are not a failure until you give up. You are not a flop until you let go. So, don't quit. Never give up. Keep going. Hold on.** God's rewards await us in the distant future not near the beginning; and we don't know how many steps it will take to reach the prize. Endurance is needed to see the end and embrace the prize. **So, fight another round, rise another time, run another mile, and, above all, don't let go and don't quit.**

It was a fog-shrouded morning, July 4, 1952, when a young woman named Florence Chadwick waded into the water off Catalina Island. She intended to swim the channel from the island to the California coast. Long-distance swimming was not new to her; she had been the first woman to swim the English Channel in both directions.

The water was numbing cold that day. The fog was so thick she could hardly see the boats in her party. Several times sharks had to be driven away with rifle fire. She swam more than 15 hours before she asked to be taken out of the water. Her trainer tried to encourage her to swim on since they were so close to land, but when Florence looked, all she saw was fog. So, she quit... only one mile from her goal.

Later she said, "I'm not excusing myself, but if I could have seen the land, I might have made it." It wasn't the cold or fear or exhaustion that caused Florence Chadwick to fail. It was the fog.

Many times, we fail, not because we're afraid or because of the peer pressure or because of anything other than the fact that we lose sight of the goal. Maybe that's why Paul said**, "I press toward the mark for the prize of the high calling of God in Christ Jesus" (Phil. 3:14). So, press on "Vision Chaser", press on.**

Chasing the Vision is your path to growth. Chasing the vision helps to answer the many eternal questions of life. How do I know if I'm on track to reaching heaven? Will I gain acceptance through the gate on judgment? The only way to know is by passing the test we have in life. The test and challenges in life gives us a chance to see the areas we need to grow and mature in. They change us and give us chances to make changes. **(James 1:5)**. The test, the experiences we have--allows us to apply what we've learned so we not only grow old, but we grow up. In order to grow, you must be looking for opportunities to grow.

With every mistake, trial, and tribulation you must gain wisdom, knowledge and understanding. It does not matter if you were the King or Queen of mess-ups. Own it, learn from it and next time follow the Word of God. When faced with temptation, you always answer with scripture, just like Jesus. **(Matthew 4:1-11).** When someone does you wrong, you should return good for evil, just as He did. **(1 Peter 2:23).** When someone is in need, show compassion. **(Matthew 14:14).** As a mature believer-you no longer dwell in the past. In order to grow you cannot waist time and energy dwelling on past mistakes and sins. You cannot chase the vision of God, while wallowing in remorse and self-pity. Bottom line, we all have sinned. **(Romans 3:23).** If you stay in the past, it will destroy you and your divine destiny. There is a goal to reach **(Colossians 3:1-4).** God rewards those who diligently seek him. **(Hebrew 11:6).** Stop beating yourself up for past mistakes. Stop giving lip service about being forgiven and just accept it. When we condemn ourselves, we are saying, "Jesus, your blood was not enough to cleanse and redeem me. **We must grow by trusting the Lord, even in unexpected storms.**

VISION SHINES BRIGHT

Let your light shine. Be the Label or Labor great or small do it well or not at all. Letting your light shine in this post pandemic world is difficult, but not impossible. You might be jobless, hopeless, and literally penniless. But if you have an internet connection, a smart phone, a good laptop or iPad and a little bit of will power, then you still have the tools necessary to Chase the Vision and let your light shine. As a Vision Chaser continues to grow during these uncertain times, the Vision that is chased shines brighter. **Isaiah 60:1** state: "Arise, **shine**, for your light has come, and the glory of the Lord has risen upon you. For behold, darkness shall cover the earth, and thick darkness the peoples; but the Lord will arise upon you, and his glory will be seen upon you." Vision Chasers it's time to **"Rise, Shine, your time has come."** Despite the many struggles and hardships of Chasing the Vision, every time people see you, they should see your **light rise and shining bright,** reflecting the Glory of God. "Then spake Jesus again unto them, saying, I am the light of the world: he that followeth me shall not walk in darkness, but shall have the light of life." **(John 8:12).**

Every morning you should wake up feeling exceptional. Because you are important, needed, and unique because the light of God shine through you and everything you do. Your business must shine by having a vision to standout. You must set goals and form strategies to reach them. Be determine to push through the difficult times. This Post pandemic era requires a love for Jesus Christ and a strong mental attitude. You must be prepared to seize opportunities when they come along. Think outside the box. Be creative so you can standout and outshine the competition. You must invest in online and offline marketing to expand your audience.

Not everybody will want to see you shine but shine anyway. We sometimes forget that in order for a candle to shine bright, it must be willing to endure burning. Some of us may even be like Glo sticks, we have to be broken before we shine. There is a new phrase that has entered our mainstream culture called "Throwing Shade." Throwing Shade is to talk negatively about, to publicly denounce or disrespect someone. It has become a new way for breaking the vision chaser and prevent us from shining. Shining means to give out or to reflect bright light. In order to continue to "Chase the Vision" you got to be able to shine while others are throwing shade at you. Because light does not cast a shadow. **You have got to keep the flame in your torch burning.** Jesus gave us the example in **John 18:37-38**. When Pilate asked him if he were a king. "You say that I am..." Jesus then says, "Everyone who belongs to the truth listens to My voice." **Verse 38** then Pilate responded, "What is truth?" There are some shady people in this world who will try to convince people that the truth is what they say it is. Shady people can't stand it when a Vision Chaser is shining. Shady people don't feel tall unless they can make you feel small. Shady people will hold you down in order to build themselves up. So, if you are at a point that you feel your light dimming, rest and recharge, knowing who you are and that your light was meant to shine in dark and shady places.

Vision Chasers are born to shine. God has handed to each of us a torch to bear for him. That torch is the light of the Gospel, the knowledge of God and His ways, and the Word of God. This light is meant to shine in ministry, in your family and in your business. Each of us are to let our light shine that all men can see Jesus in us and then we are told to run with it and to pass it on to the next generation so that they will not forget God.

Fannie Lou Hamer was one of the Ambassadors and Torch Bearers of the Civil Rights movement. On June 9, 1963, she experienced some shade in the midst of a season that God was permitting her an opportunity to shine. While returning from a voter registration workshop in South Carolina, Fannie Lou Hamer and other civil rights activists were arrested in Winona, Mississippi. It was a time when segregation and discrimination were major topics in America. Ms. Hamer and the other activists had been traveling in the "white" section of a Greyhound bus despite threats from the driver that he planned to notify local police at the next stop. When the bus arrived at the Winona bus depot, the activists sat at the "white only" lunch counter inside the terminal. Winona Police Chief, Thomas Herrod, ordered the group to go to the "colored" side of the depot and arrested them when one of the activists tried to write down his patrol car license number. Instead of protesting, Fannie started singing, "This little light of mine. I'm gone let it shine. Everywhere I go, I'm gonna let it shine. Let it Shine, let it shine. Let it shine." She was going to jail, not church, and she's singing, "This little light of mine—I'm gonna let it shine."

Fannie is brutally and savagely beaten and sexually assaulted while in custody by some shady people who did not want her light to shine. Can you imagine getting beaten just because you wanted your light to shine. Just because you wanted to help somebody.

Just because you wanted to make your community better. Just because you wanted to fulfill the outreach ministry of the bible to feed the hungry, clothe the naked, visit the sick and those in prison, to educate the uneducated and to love the unlovable. All she was trying to do was be a light to the world. She was pursuing her vision for equality while everyone around her was determined to extinguish her flame.

Jesus called His disciples the light of the world, living testimonies of Christ's goodness, revealing, and illuminating the truth. Isaiah and other prophets used it as a symbol of hope-something John the Baptist and the gospel writers picked up. In the first century, long before electricity, light was rare and expensive. People in Jesus' day were used to living in the dark, because the oil or fat needed to fuel a lamp was considered a luxury. But just a little light could go a long way. As Jesus says, just one little lamp properly placed, could light an entire home.

We, like the early gospel community, struggle to shine our light. We hide it under bushels of fear. We dissolve it in conflict. We refuse to go forward with our visions and dreams because we feel we don't have the proper support from the people in our circle. But if you got the redeemer then you have all the resources you need.

In this polarized world we live in, it seems that Christians today are more comfortable throwing shade on others than shining the light of Christ. As a result, we are not shining our light to a world in darkness. We are not proclaiming God's kingdom-God's eternal reign of love and peace. *Mahatma Gandhi declared, "I'd be a Christian if it were not for the Christians!" I like your Christ, I do not like your Christians."*

These questions force us to ask ourselves: how are we to live in community? How are we to shine the light of God's Kingdom without fear into our world? **How can I be a successful business owner and be a Christian at the same time? How can I serve in Senior Management and even be President of a Company and not sacrifice my faith and belief in Jesus Christ?** I do so by implementing God's word and Christian principals in life, ministry, and business. God made you. So do you! Nothing will upset your haters more than for you to do or accomplish that which they thought you shouldn't or couldn't and you do it right in front of them. Go ahead and upset them. Go ahead and rock the boat. No matter what your past—your heart ache and pain— Chase the Vision. Don't let people who don't have a heaven or hell to put you in stop you from serving God and giving God praise by using all of your gifts and talents. Let nothing be held over head. Because whatever is over you, defines you and whatever defines you, limits you.

We know that God is omnipresent, that wherever we are—God is there. And wherever God is, there is light - even in darkness. Vision Chaser it's time for you to shine like God, even in darkness. Despite the Biblical truth, a lot of believers still have that **hymnal faith.** When I was growing up, we had hymnals on every pew in the Church. There's was a stamp on the inside of the cover of the hymnal— **"not to be removed from Church."** A lot of us treat God that way, not to be removed from Church, we exit church and leave God behind. But when you go home—God should go with you. When you go to work—God should go with you.

When God goes with you, He sets you free. Adam Clayton Powell words are still true. "Freedom is not an external adjustment, but an internal achievement." Jesus has delivered you from your inside man. You are set free. Free from the opinion of other people. Free from the noise of the crowd. Free to worship in Spirit and in Truth. Free from the demons that have tormented you for years. Free from the chains and burdens that have held you bound. Free from injustice. Free from the hurt and pain caused by your past—even if it was self-inflicted.

So, let your light shine.

REFLECTIONS

There is no greater witness than a born-again believer, an Ambassador for Christ, reflecting the light of the Lord Jesus Christ. It is such a powerful testimony when a life, a ministry, a business displays the proof of His presence through the fruit of the spirit. **Gal. 5:22-23.** Vision Chasers don't have to audition for God! He has already given you the role. Just remember to learn and do your part. Everything about you should reflect Jesus Christ. For example, your Household budget should reflect Jesus Christ. Before paying your mortgage or rent, you should tithe. Your Business should tithe. Your Ministry should reflect the Jesus Christ by investing in Community Outreach and Evangelism. As a Vision Chaser, you have got to stand up and let your light shine, because you reflect your Savior. As an Ambassador and Future Torch Bearer you should reflect the Visionary. The employees of every business should be trained not only for the skilled positions, but also on how to be Ambassadors and Future Torch Bearers for the vision of the Owner. We were born into sin and shaped in iniquity from the dirt of the earth. Thus, in order to project your Vision to the world, you must reflect the spirit of God. **Colossians 4:17** "And say to Archippus, take heed to the ministry which thou has received in the Lord, that thou fulfill it." You can only fulfill the ministry, the vision, the dream, the mission by reflecting the spirit of God. Again, Jesus spoke to them, saying, "I am the light of the world. Whoever follows me will not walk in darkness, but will have the light of life," **John 8:12.** Jesus reflects God. To see Jesus is to see God. When people see you, they should also see Christ.

This truth is seen in the witness of the Gadarene Demoniac living in the cemetery in **Mark 5:1-20** and through the witness of the woman at the well, **John 4:39.** When light hits an object, that light will either be absorbed or reflected. If you are a Christian Business entrepreneur, your business should reflect Jesus Christ. Reflection means to give back an image or likeness. Reflection is when light bounces off an object. Light reflects from a smooth surface at the same angle as it hits the surface. For a smooth surface, reflected light rays travel in the same direction. This is called specular reflection. For a rough surface, reflected light rays scatter in all directions. This is called diffuse reflection. Visionaries that are reflecting the light of Christ's reflection is diffused. **It doesn't matter from what direction life meets you, they will see the reflection of God and the Vision you are chasing.** Most of the things we see are because light from a source has reflected off it.

Water is also a reflective surface. When a Vision Chaser is reflecting the Living Water (Jesus) even though we may face some rough times, trials and tribulations, and storms and wind may blow—the reflection of the image of God is still there. Reflection is important if we are to learn from the past and be a witness in the present and future. A glass mirror reflects physical light whereas God's mirror (the Word of God) reflects spiritual light. Whether we are polished, mature Christians or rough around the edges, we are still capable of reflecting God's light.

In Business we reflect the spirit of God by making our bottom line about eternity with Jesus and not just profit. For example:

1. The Business objective is to make disciples of Jesus Christ by using principals that reflect the character of Jesus.
2. You treat your customers, employees, clients, stakeholders as Jesus would.
3. God's presence is felt as the company is led by the voice and power of the Holy Spirit.
4. Visionaries in business should be like Moses when he was leading the Children of Israel toward the promise land. Moses said to God, "If your Presence does not go with us, do not send us up from here." **(Exodus 33:15)**.
5. You seek Godly counsel and are accountable. The Bible says, "where there is no guidance the people fall, but in abundance of counselors there is victory." **(Proverbs 11:14).**
6. **Tithe—** "and you shall remember the Lord your God, for it is He who gives you power to get wealth, that He may establish His covenant which He swore to your fathers, as it is this day." **(Deuteronomy 8:18).**
7. Love people and use money.
8. Let your business be based on uncompromising and unapologetic Christian Biblical principles.

God decides how He will use us as Vision Chasers and whatever He chooses we should do it in such a way that it brings Him Honor. It's God's vision – and if the vision is in ministry, He may choose to use you for specular reflection – very targeted to a specific person, group, place, or time. Or He may choose to use you across a larger and broader way (more diffusely

Vision Chasers, I want to challenge you. I need you to begin to look in the mirror and start thanking God for who you are about to become. Over 700,000 people have died as a result of Covid 19, but you are still counted amongst the living. You are the visible evidence that Christ still reigns supreme. So, take a moment to thank God that you are still breathing and do not take His grace and mercy for granted. Be steadfast in the Word of God. He has a great purpose for your life. When you look in the mirror it should remind you just how valuable and precious you are to God.

Dr. Michael Eric Dyson in his work titled, "Tears we cannot Stop" insightfully and transparently speaks of the internal predicament of his father living during the civil rights movement. He said his father had become a prisoner of disbelief in his own worth and purpose. **It is a fact that if you don't know your own worth—you allow people to get you at a discount.** Dr. Dyson teaches us that you don't have to be in prison to be a prisoner. You don't have to be in jail—to be locked up. His dad had become handcuffed by helplessness. His spirit had become shackled and as a consequence he was a prisoner of disbelief in his own worth and purpose. He was unable to reflect God's purpose for his life.

All Vision Chasers have had some moments when we were shackled by self-doubt and handcuffed by helplessness in our pursuit of the Vision. The enemy will always try to use people and situations to distract you from your purpose. Remember Simba—the star of the Disney movie "The Lion King"? Simba had allowed his Uncle Scar to get into his head. As believers, we must be careful not to allow the enemy to get into our head; because they will get in your head and sabotage your spirit and handcuff your hope. **Hope is not an emotion; it is a decision. Decide, to never give up your hope.** If you give the enemy access to your mind, it will affect your decision-making abilities. Simba is told by Scar that he is responsible for the death of Mufasa, his father. But

Scar is a hater. He hates on Simba because he is still wounded by the fact that Mufasa had become King instead of him. A physical scar is evidence of a wound that is healed. However, the physical scars sometimes leaves us with emotional scars. Because of his hatred for Simba and his unhealed wounds from Mufasa, Scar kills Mufasa and blames Simba. Scar said, "he was the one who started the stampede that killed Mufasa." The enemy will always throw rocks and hide his/her hands, claiming that they are innocent. They will even confess that their hands are clean. The enemy will try anything if he/she believes it will make you stop Chasing the Vision of your destiny. At one point, Simba was singing, "I just can't wait to be King." Now because Scar has gotten into his head Simba is no longer Chasing the Vision of his destiny, but he is running away from it. He is trying to run away from his past. He has allowed his past to order the steps of his present by hanging out with a Mire Cat and a Wort Hog singing "A Cuna Matata". **He is living with no worries, but he is supposed to be King (the Future Torch Bearer), and Kings have a responsibility to lead.**

What are you supposed to be in the Kingdom? Why are you in hiding? Why have you walked away? Why are you no longer Chasing the Vision of destiny? Who told you to run away? Who told you God was done with you? Who did you give your hope to?

Simba has run away and is now living beneath his possibilities. Darla finds him and informs him of how much Scar has damaged the herd and the pride lands. Sometimes when we run away, we forget about the people we left behind. We forget that if we would step into our destiny—things would change for the better. Finally, Rafiki the baboon comes along and hits him on the head. It is times like these you need to pray that God sends a Rafiki in your life and hits you on the head. Rafiki hits Simba on the head and Simba says ouch, what you do that for? Rafiki tells him, it doesn't matter, it's in the past. Simba says, yeah but it still hurts. I know past mistakes hurt. But we must remember that when we have sinned against or offended others the answer is confession, repentance, and forgiveness. The answer is never retreat or exile. Forgiveness is at the very foundation of our Christian faith. Without forgiveness we would not have salvation by faith. However, it seems sometimes that Christians are the most unforgiving people...and as James said, "...My brethren, these things ought not so to be." **(3:10). These things do not reflect Jesus Christ.**

Simba's problem was not forgiving himself **(which is impossible)** it was allowing Scar **(the enemy)** access to his mind. I don't know what's in your past. But I will understand if you tell me, it still hurts or that you still have scars and unhealed wounds. I do understand. People will bring up your past, especially if it will further their present personal agenda. But you must remember that the rock of your salvation still lives on the inside of you. That's why Rafiki tells Simba—Mufasa still lives. Your destiny still awaits you. When he says that, Simba is energized with expectation. Simba realizes that he is the **Future Torch Bearer** and **Visionary**. Simba goes to the water and looks at a **reflection in the water.** He says, that's not Mufasa—that's just me. He then has a Vision. In this Vision, Mufasa appears and says, "Simba you have forgotten me, **remember who you are, you are more than what you have become."** When you look in the mirror don't just see your reflection but see God **(your heavenly father)** inside of you. Stop running away and start pursuing the Vision God gave you of your destiny. None of us want God to judge us for not chasing and pursuing our destiny. No one wants to stand before God and hear God say, "you were created to be more than what you have become." No one wants to hear God say, "depart from me, you worker of iniquity." All of us want to hear God say, "well done thy good and faithful servant."

Now is the moment in your life where it is necessary to look at where you are as opposed to where you should be. **Is God saying—that you are more than what you have become?** Why was Simba more than what he had become? To quote Dr. Dyson, **Simba had become a prisoner of disbelief in his own worth.** He was not reflecting the character instilled in him by his father. He had convinced himself that everyone was better off without him because of what had happened in his past. Relationships were better off—if he wasn't in them. People were better off if he was not the one in leadership. He had become bitter like most of us due to unforgiveness. The enemy forces us to keep turning over and over the hurt in our mind. It's a vicious cycle that causes a bitter person to always be angry about something. It's a trick of the enemy to keep you in bondage to past mistakes and past hurt. If we don't forgive, we will always live in some past hurt, because we constantly re-live it in our minds. It keeps us living in guilt and pain causing a person to become sick physically, mentally, and spiritually.

Reflecting God requires us to forgive. We must forgive others and accept the forgiveness of God for our own sin. We must stop being the victim and sincerely pray for those who have hurt us. It's very difficult to be angry or unforgiving towards a person whom you are earnestly praying for! If you need an example just look to God. **Could you forgive someone who killed your only son?**

God did. He does not allow the sin to be remembered anymore. We look to Jesus as an example. When He was hanging on the cross experiencing the worst pain a person could experience, while the blood was dripping down His hands and His flesh was tearing at the nails. He said, "Father, forgive them, for they know not what they do." If Jesus could forgive us, we should be able to forgive those who have hurt us and accept His forgiveness for our own transgressions. It was our sins that nailed Him to the tree: your sins and mine. As believers in Jesus Christ, we should be **Ambassadors** of kindness. We should, "put away all malice and all guile and insincerity and envy and all slander for you have tasted the kindness of the Lord." **(1 Peter 2:1-3). Kindness is the honey of the fruit of the spirit.**

We serve a kind and forgiving God. Thus, we must be kind and forgiving as well. The root of His love is forgiveness. How we view forgiveness will affect our relationship with Him, and with those around us. If we wish to be spiritually healthy, if we wish to be free from condemnation, then we must forgive ourselves for the hurt and pain we caused. **We must find the root of our SCARS, so, we can adequately reflect the spirit of God and chase the vision.**

VISION CHASERS ARE CRAZY

My little Business is going to be a big Business one day! My family shall prosper financially! My ministry shall win souls for God's kingdom! Yeah, I said it! And I'm crazy enough to believe it! You have to believe in your business plan, your vision, and your family goals even when no one else does. You have to have crazy faith even when you are surrounded by doubt.

Some people will look at you strange because you are striving to expand or start a business in the midst of a pandemic. **They might even call you crazy!** Vision Chasers who are reflecting the light of Jesus Christ have to have the right mind set and that mind set is crazy! **Vision Chasers strive (or live) off stretch goals, big plans, and even bigger dreams.** Vision Chasers are crazy for Jesus! Visionaries are called crazy for thinking and believing the impossible. Ambassadors are called crazy for being co-signers and representatives of the visionary's crazy train of thinking. Future Torch Bearers are called crazy for wanting to continue and then build upon such a crazy vision. Even Jesus was called crazy which means His disciples must have been crazy to follow him and continue his work. "Then [Jesus} went home; and the crowd came together again, so that they could not even eat. When his family heard it, they went out to restrain him, for people were saying, "He has gone out of his mind." **(Mark 3:19-21).** "Jesus has gone out of his mind." That's what the people said in the New Revised Standard Version of the Bible. The King James Version translates it as, "He is beside himself." The Contemporary English Version says, "When Jesus' family heard what he was doing, they thought he was crazy and went to get him under control. Jesus was reflecting the light of His father and people thought He was crazy.

I declare, if you are going to be a Vision Chaser—you have got to be a little crazy. You have got to be one of those Christians who are crazy enough to grasp the transforming, transfiguring, life-changing vision of Jesus Christ our Savior and follow Him in faith until the very end. It doesn't matter what anyone else has to say or think. It doesn't matter if you are chasing the vision in business, family, or ministry. You have to be a little crazy to walk by faith. Because our faith makes no sense to the world. The Bible says in **Hebrews 11** that without faith it is impossible to please God. If you want to please God, you've got to be crazy. You've got to be out of your mind to have the mind of Christ. You've got to be crazy to believe in the Cross, and the Death, Salvation and Resurrection of Jesus Christ! **So, why not have a crazy vision.** The Word says, let this mind be in you which is also in Christ Jesus. So, has someone told you your vision is crazy? Has someone told you they didn't think your business idea would be successful? If you are a business owner, you have to be a little crazy to follows the words of **Matthew Chapter 6**, "You can't serve both God and money." You have to be crazy to operate a business and put the love of people over profits. **Now profit is good. More profit more mission but profit never trump mission.** If you sincerely chase the vision of God, at some point people will deem you to be crazy. Vision craziness causes you to stretch your faith to believe God for things you can't see, because you know what He promised. Believe it even when nobody else can—simply because, like Caleb and Joshua when they spied out the promise land, you know God is able. There is a degree of foolishness about chasing a Vision that sometimes no one else can see other than you and God, but its ok. **1 Corinthians 1:18** states: "For the message of the cross is foolishness to those who are perishing, but to us who are being saved it is the power of God!"

Vision Chasers are always having conversations with the Holy Spirit—so people call you crazy. **Vision Chasers can discern in the spirt and see ahead of people. They see what others don't see.** So, they call you crazy. The direction God is giving you during this Post Pandemic season, there have been times even you thought—this is foolishness. You received the vision to start, open or grow in the midst of quarantine and business closures or keep church doors open. People will think you are crazy, because even though they know you are struggling—they always see you smiling. When your wisdom has dried up, you've got to have some crazy faith. When you are in the middle of a storm—it takes crazy faith to believe that God is going to step in and calm the sea and tell the wind to behave. You have to be crazy to believe that with everything that happens to you in this life, God is going to work it out for your good.

Several years back, there was a man swimming on the shores of South Carolina and out of nowhere a storm came. The news reported: "Man saved by shark". When I saw the headline—I said, I've got to see this, because that's crazy. Apparently, while the man was swimming, he was bitten by a shark, and he couldn't get away. So, he started calling on the name of Jesus and screaming with all that was within him. He started hitting the shark. He hit the shark in the eye and again in the nose. He hit the shark so hard that the shark had to let him go. Meanwhile, once he was rescued and taken to the hospital, the doctor in the ER opened up his wounds and told him that there was a cancerous growth on his kidney and if the cancer had not been removed during that surgery, he would have been dead in just a few months. His testimony was-the shark bit me—but the shark saved me. Vision Chasers have some crazy testimonies. You might be swimming with the sharks, living next to sharks, in business with sharks, even worshipping every Sunday with sharks, but know that all things work together for the good of them that are called according to His purpose.

Vision Chaser, you are the light of the world, and your light works best, not in the sunlight of the church, but in the darkness of the world. Vision Chasers will always have that desire to do community outreach, evangelize and witness to their community—to work outside the walls of traditional church. Almost all of the miracles Jesus performed he did them outside the walls of the Church. He fed the 5000 outside. He healed all the blind men—outside. He healed those who were crippled at the pool of Bethesda—outside. He led the march on Jerusalem—outside. He healed the sick—outside. You do know where He was when they nailed Him to the cross? He was Outside. The Bible says, He got up early Sunday morning with all power in His hand---You know where He was standing when Mary and Martha came to the tomb? He was outside. Crazy faith says, we believe that He is coming back, and He is going to meet us in the middle of the air—you know where that is? Outside. If you are called to be a Vision Chaser, you better get used to working outside the traditions of the Church and outside normal business practices. Because to the traditionalist, you will seem crazy.

You have to be crazy to turn the other cheek, to give away your cloak when you are sued for your tunic, or to go the extra mile. But my God says I must and I'm crazy enough to do it. There's more you have to be a little crazy to follow **Matthew 5:38-48 and** love people when they are trying to cause you intentional harm. **Verse 44** specifically states, "But I say unto you, Love your enemies, bless them that curse you, do good to them that hate you, and pray for them which despitefully use you, and persecute you;" You've got to be crazy to keep doing the will of God despite the treatment you receive from the world and sometimes even from the children of God. It's been said, "the people who are crazy enough to think they can change the world, are the ones who do." So, how crazy are you?

You can't be successful as a Vision Chaser acting like you are sane, being program driven, only operating in your comfort zone. In this post pandemic world, you cannot launch a successful new enterprise using traditional methods. Technology must become your new friend. Even ministry and worship have to be different. You have to become a party crasher like Mary Magdalene and be crazy enough to believe in healing and deliverance in the 20th century. Crazy enough to believe that Christians should still be concerned about leading lost souls to Jesus Christ as Savior, feeding the hungry, clothing the naked, and create affordable housing and equal access to capital.

Vision Chasers are faith walkers. They have a "Spirit of Excellence". Vision Chasers are "Water Walkers". Like Peter in **Matthew 14**. They are people who are not afraid to get out of the boat and do what has never been done. They are not waiting for permission. They don't need the Pastor or the CEO of the company to be the only one to cast vision. They can see God and hear God calling them. They can see greatness and potential and take the initiative to step out into new things.

Vision Chasers believe that following Jesus means changing the world from the nightmare it often is into the dream that God promised. Vision Chasers march to the beat of a different drummer. It means caring more when you really want to care less. It means standing up when others are sitting down. It is recognizing the necessity to be the voice for the voiceless. It means speaking out when others are shutting up. If you are crazy for Jesus that means you are going to have some people that will be in your camp, that are not really in your corner. Yes, people are going to talk about you. They talked about Jesus. His own family called Him crazy. But Jesus didn't allow their issue with Him—to become an issue for Him. They might see your worship and praise and call you crazy. They might see you stand on the Word and confess your faith and call you crazy. Don't worry because Vision Chasers are crazy--crazy for Jesus!

You've got to be able to tell people—don't judge my expression if you don't know my experience. **If you don't know my hell, stay out my halleluiah.** If you've never been me, don't judge me. Vision Chasers are different because our Savior is different. You are truly a peculiar person, set apart by God to do something **extraordinary** for the Kingdom. **1 Peter 2:9** states, "But you are a chosen people, a royal priesthood, a holy nation. **Deut. 14:2** says, you have been set apart as holy unto God. **Romans 12:2** says, do not be conformed unto this world, but be ye transformed by the renewing of your mind. **Galatians 2:20** says, my old self has been crucified with Christ. It is no longer I who live, but Christ lives in me.

Steve Jobs is a good example of a "Vision Chaser". Steve Jobs was one of the founders of Apple Inc., the company that just improved its net worth to over a Trillion dollars. After his death, an old Apple, Inc. commercial went viral on YouTube. It was a commercial that's goal had been to rebrand Apple products. The tag line for the commercial and for the company was: Think different. In the commercial they showed a collage of photographs and film footage of people who have invented, inspired creativity, and sacrificed to improve the world, to make a difference. They showed Bob Dylan, Amelia Earhart, Frank Lloyd Wright, Maria Callas, Muhammad Ali, Martin Luther King, Jr., Jim Henson, Mother Teresa, Albert Einstein, Pablo Casals, Mahatma Gandhi, Albert Schweitzer, and numerous others. As the images rolled by a poem was narrated:

Here's to the crazy ones. The misfits. The rebels. The troublemakers. The round pegs in the square holes. The ones who see things differently. They're not fond of rules. And they have no respect for the status quo. You can quote them, disagree with them, glorify, or vilify them. About the only thing you can't do is ignore them. Because they change things. They invent. They imagine. They heal. They explore. They create. They inspire. They push the human race forward. Maybe they have to be crazy. How else can you stare at an empty canvas and see a work of art? Or sit in silence and hear a song that's never been written? Or gaze at a red planet and see a laboratory on wheels? While some see them as the crazy ones, we see genius. Because the people who are crazy enough to think they can change the world, are the ones who do.

Vision Chasers are those who would dare to become the salt of the World. Like natural salt—you're not going to make an impact unless you make some contact. If you are determined to continue this journey of Chasing the Vision God has placed before you and within you—then its time you become a little crazy. **Be like Noah. He didn't stop building the ark to explain himself to every doubter and hater. He kept building and let the rain do all the talking.**

KEEP CHASING THE VISION

Every morning you have two choices: Keep sleeping with your dreams or wake up and chase them. So what, people think you are crazy, despite the obstacles, the cost, and many setbacks, you keep chasing and moving forward. You can't let anything distract you from pursuing the call God has on your life. God is giving you a unique opportunity to be listed among the great heroes of the faith and the greatest entrepreneurs of our time. You have to be determined to make a mark on the world and not let the world make a mark on you. You are a headlight -- not a taillight. You are a leader not a follower. You can't let every problem of the people become your problem. You are not a camel. You can help people without carrying them on your back. Because how many folks can you carry before you fall? How many battles can you fight before you have no fight left? God has many warriors and vision chasers, and they are called to do different things for the Kingdom. Find your passion, your lane and keep running toward your destiny and not away from it.

In **1 Kings 18**, Elijah was spiritually discouraged when he ran from Jezebel. As he crosses the desert, trying to get as far away from her threats, he prays for death to come upon him. He tells God he has had enough. An angel provides him with food and water, as he continued his journey. Then he meets God at the cave of Horeb and God asks the all-important question, "What are you doing here, Elijah?" If you read this story, you will find Elijah answers God in what I believe is sort of a whiney, beat-down, totally discouraged, and disheartened voice. He tells God, and I'm paraphrasing a bit loosely, "I've been really on fire for you, Lord, but I'm the only one left. Nobody else is serving you and the task is just too big for me to do alone!" God then tells him that even though he feels alone there are thousands who have remained faithful and instructs Elijah to keep chasing the vision.

In the midst of this walk of faith what's going to be your next step? Because God is not through with you! Your Chasing days are not over, they have only just begun. **God is using you for a great work and if your path seems to be more difficult than others its only because your calling is higher.** One thing the pandemic has shown us is that Chasing the Vision is not about going to church or having church, but it's about being the Church. All of us have experienced some hurt and pain that has knocked us down. For some people, it was so devasting that emotionally you feel you are not able to get up. You feel as if your dreams have been kidnapped by a nightmare. Some have experienced defeat and disappointment. Choices have been made that have had dire consequences. But here is the good news of the gospel–Jesus still reigns supreme. You still have Vision therefore, you have purpose. For a people without a vision will perish. **Sometimes God allows life to knock us down—so we can look up, get up and reposition ourselves for a new vision and a new purpose.**

You are a Just Man or Woman. And even just men and women fall short of the glory of God. But what makes them **just** is that they get back up again. If a Vision Chaser falls down 7 times, you should get up 8. Because **the ground is no place for a champion**. Champions get tired, get winded, and even discouraged but they don't quit. When one gets tired of Chasing the Vision—it becomes easy for us to fall short of the powerful disciplined sanctified church we saw in the Book of Acts. Instead of preaching the good news that sinners can be made righteous in Christ, we have settled for a "gospel" that implies that God's primary purpose in saving us is to unfold a "wonderful plan" for our lives, to solve our problems, make us happy, and rescue us from the hassles of life. But truth be told—walking by faith is hard work. This is consistent with scriptures admonishing us to count the cost for following Jesus and Chasing Visions. "If they persecuted Me, they would also persecute you" **(John 15:20)**; "In this world you will have tribulations **(John 16:33)**; "We must go through many tribulations before we can enter the Kingdom of God" **(Acts 14:22)**. The promise of the gospel—doing the will of God, Chasing the Vision of God has never been one of an enhanced life on earth. During our journey we are to forsake all that we have, deny ourselves, and take up the cross daily and follow him. **(2 Timothy 3:2)**. Jesus warned those who followed him that the time would come when people would murder them, (physically and spiritually) and think they were doing God a favor by spilling their blood **(John 16:2)**. All of your attackers and haters—first had to justify in their minds—that the death of you, destruction of your family, your ministry or your business was their life's work.

In **Mark 8:24**, Jesus says, "whoever wants to be my disciple must deny themselves and take up their cross and follow me." **(See also Luke 9:23, Matthew 16:24)**. Jesus was calling his followers to deny themselves the world's paltry, brief joys that they might have overflowing eternal joy; to deny themselves hell that they might have heaven. He went on to say: For whoever would save his life will lose it, but whoever loses his life for my sake and the gospel's will save it. We accomplish this daily by recognizing that God has left us here for a purpose. That purpose is to bring glory to Christ. Paul called this **"Pressing toward the mark."** It is personal, no one is going to do it for you. No matter the attacks from the enemy, you have to keep pressing in the name of Jesus.

God has called you to run a long-distance race of faith. That's why Paul wrote, do you not know that in a race all the runners run, but only one receives the prize? So, run that you might obtain it. Every athlete exercises self-control in all things. They do it to receive a perishable wreath, but we are imperishable. So, I do not run aimlessly...[but] I discipline my body and keep it under control, lest after preaching to others I myself should be disqualified. **(1 Corinthians 9:24-27).** In order to continue the chase with strength and power you must distance yourself from those things that weigh on your heart, entangle your feet, put distracting noise in your head, and deplete your energy. God has given you a unique vision to chase—and He has equipped you to achieve it. Remember that whatever does not proceed in faith—is sin. **Romans 14:23.** And God has assigned to each of us the measure of faith needed to Chase the Vision. **When you stand before God on judgment, He is not going to ask you about my vision. He is going to ask you about yours.** Thus, you must pray to make sure you know what the will of God is for you **(Ephesians 5:17) and** be content with the race (vision) you've been given. **(Hebrews 13:5).** Focus hard on how to win it. Know that laying aside the weight of sin---isn't a one-time thing, it is a daily thing. **It's a skill acquired through constant practice.**

If you are going to keep moving forward, you have to learn how to **recover from failure**. It's hard to recover from what feels like a losing battle, but you must. It's hell to keep walking by faith into a door of disappointment. You know you are doing the work of the Lord, but it feels like you're fighting a losing battle. It's a true fact that it doesn't matter how saved you are or how big your bible is or how often you go to church—people of faith catch hell every day, especially when you trying to fulfill the vision. But a Vision Chaser would still rather catch hell catching fish for Christ, then to catch HELL for eternity.

In 2017 Muhammad Ali died. I couldn't help but go back and read up on the "GOAT" the greatest of all times. When Ali died, USA Today ran a full-page article and in the center of the page they featured George Forman and "Rumble in the Jungle". George was the Heavy Weight Champ and favored to win. But Ali came out floating like a butterfly and stinging like a bee. He introduced a new fighting style called the "rope-a-dope". George had beaten Joe Frazier and destroyed Ken Norton and was picked by the media to defeat Ali. But in round 4, Ali is in his corner, and he is talking smack to George. He has become the **noise** in George's head. George was hitting Ali with punches that had defeated Frazier and Norton, punches that had landed him the Gold in the Olympics and the Heavy Weight belt. But after all the punches, Ali was still standing.

When you are chasing the Vision, you will often question yourself when what you used to do does not work anymore. When the prayer, rebuking, fasting, reading, and studying that worked during your last fight, doesn't' work. When the business plan doesn't work because it didn't consider a global pandemic, quarantine, and social distancing. During the fight, George is giving it all he's got—but Ali is talking to George. Ali said, "is that all you got, my mama hits harder than you." George is quoted in the documentary, "Facing Ali" that in round 4-when Ali said, "is that all you got." George said, I remembered saying, "yeah that's all I got." And I'm getting tired of swinging and having no affect. I know you have been there (having doubt) and might even be in that situation right now. Peter was on the boat saying I've cast this net all night and I have not caught anything. I'm tired. I just want to quit, clean my net, and go home.

George lost the fight in round 8 but he really lost the fight in round 4, not from the ring, but from the corner. He was defeated internally long before he was defeated externally. Some Vision Chasers are defeated right now. You're still in church working in ministry, but you are defeated. You're still throwing punches for Jesus, but you have been defeated. All because you let the enemy get into your head. Jesus even said, your prayers cannot even be answered if you pray in doubt. George was in doubt by round 4 and in round 8, he goes down. In round 8 George goes down Ali wins and everybody in the crowd shouts Ali! In the documentary— "When We Were Kings" They show George exiting the ring—alone. He came with a group, but he leaves by himself. When you're winning everybody is with you. When you lose, you lose alone. My college coach once said, Victory has many mothers, but failure is an orphan. It's amazing how losing, loss, failure, and defeat exposes who your real friends are. George is walking away in defeat and alone because he allowed his enemy to get into his head. **(Stop the noise).**

When the enemy gets in your head, the noise will make you stop ministering, stop singing, stop praying, stop leading, quit your job and give up on dreams. The noise will cause you to be defeated by demons you used to defeat. The noise will cause you to lose your peace and joy, because you have been convinced that you no longer have what it takes to stand during this season. You have let this pandemic defeat you. Did you forget? Christianity is warfare. Christianity is confrontational. You can't defeat something that you won't even stand up to. Vision Chasers are being defeated because you can see the enemy but wont rebuke the enemy. You sit back and allow the enemy to defeat you with psychological warfare. The enemy has convinced you that you can't win. You quote, that you are more than a conquer, but you don't really believe it.

In the text, Peter and his crew had experienced failure in their fishing co-op. They have cast their nets and they don't just experience failure; they are on a losing streak. But Jesus got on the boat and transported them from failure to faith. Peter and his men went from a job to a call into ministry. The people were pressing Jesus, so he called Peter over in his empty boat. **It is because his boat is empty that he now has room for Jesus.** Every now and then, God will empty your life of the things you thought you had to have in order to make room for Him. Jesus steps into the empty boat and began to teach. If you're to finish this Vision Chase, you need to ask the Lord to Empty you. Empty me Lord so I can be filled with you. Because he is empty, Peter allows Jesus to use what is his. Peter said Lord this in my boat that God has blessed me with. So, I'm going to use what I've been blessed with, so the gospel can go forth in the community. It is a picture of stewardship at its best. When you recognize what God has blessed you with is not about you, the Vision to serve others will become clear. Life as a Christian, life as a Vision Chaser is not about what you get or have, but it's about what you give. **Vision Chasers are givers.**

So, Peter gives his boat, so Jesus can teach the Word. He gave everything that he had because of what he believed. That's what Colin Kaepernick did when he **took a knee** during the singing of the national anthem. The Kaepernick T-shirt for Nike says, **"Believe in something, even if it means sacrificing everything."** If you are truly going to run this race to the end, you have to believe in it enough to risk everything. Peter risked everything because he believed he had nothing to lose. That's what happened to George Forman. His story doesn't end with the Rumble in the Jungle. George after that fight hit rock bottom. But that's where he learned that Jesus will be your rock at the bottom. George began his climb back to the top—on empty. He reclaimed the title that he had lost. But God blessed him with more. It was while he was at the bottom, that George met Jesus, accepted his call into ministry of the gospel and established his own church. He got more. He is now famous for the "George Forman Grill".

Don't let your disappointments and failures stop you, **"Keep Chasing the Vision!"** God will use the failures and the disappointments to reestablish you. It's dirty work, but somebody got to do it. God has called and ordained you—to **Chase the Vision and do the Dirty Work.**

DIRTY WORK

As a Vision Chaser you can write the vision. You can share the vision with others, but if you are not willing to be an active participant in the actual work to accomplish it your vision will not manifest. **Dirty work is the actual physical hands-on work necessary to implement the vision.** Everybody wants to be successful, but nobody wants to get their hands dirty. I've had the pleasure of speaking to several people who would tell me their dreams and visions of opening a business, starting a ministry, or writing a book. I have talked to those same people one, two, three years later and they have made no forward progress. Somewhere along the way they discovered that Vision Chasing is hard dirty work. It does not matter if you are a Visionary, an Ambassador or Future Torch Bearer, at some point you are going to have to get your hands dirty. Most people think being a small business owner is glamorous. The reality is that the hardest working people in America are those people who work for themselves. Operating a small business can be stressful, overwhelming, and exhausting. But if you keep God first, He will give you strength to endure and succeed.

Similarly, the role of pastorship is idealized. According to Eugene Peterson: Being a Pastor is a taking out-the-laundry and changing-the-dirty diaper kind of job. As a pastor, you've got to be willing to take people as they are. Your time is not your own. Ministry is often discouraging, unrewarding and frustrating but as a Vision Chaser you must become content with that. **Ministry will never be glamourous because it will never be about you.**

In ministry everybody wants to be in leadership, but very few want to lead by example or lead without a title. Thus, the church at large today is afflicted with a serious unemployment problem: not of people looking for work but of work looking for people. **No one is willing to get their hands dirty.** When this happens, the vision is impoverished, and growth is stunted. However, when church unemployment is low, Hell gets nervous. Demons trembling because there is an army on the battlefield **doing the dirty work.**

Luke 10:1-3 gives us a picture of this church unemployment problem I described. After this the Lord appointed seventy-two other **(Ambassadors)** and sent them two by two ahead of him to every town and place where he was about to go. He told them, "The harvest is plentiful, but the workers are few. Ask the Lord of the harvest, therefore, to send out **workers** into his harvest field. Go! I am sending you out like lambs among wolves." Jesus said you've got to get out of your comfort zone, get your hands dirty and go out into the world and spread the gospel and yes it may even be dangerous. Paul's advice to Timothy about the work of ministry was: **2 Timothy 4:5 (NLT)** But you should keep a clear mind in every situation. Don't be afraid of suffering for the Lord. **Work** at telling others the Good News, and fully carry out the ministry God has given you.

God has called Vision Chasers because somebody has got to do the dirty work. Nothing of value happens without effort. Talk doesn't get things done. In this modern era, ministry and business requires spiritual insight, physical labor, administrative and technical skills. Vision Chasers spend so much time with staff and budget, boards, programs, groups, websites, and social media until some days we don't know which way is up. We have to take care of the leadership and managerial functions. Members and employees look at us to make sure that every I is dotted, and every T is crossed.

Vision Chasers in ministry have to do the dirty work of cleaning the Lord's house (your temple) and making it look like a house that belongs to God. Then we can do the same for the people we are leading. **2 Timothy 2:15** "Be diligent to present yourself approved to God, a worker who does not need to be ashamed, not rightly dividing the Word of truth." All too often we spend so much time on the administrative and technical functions of ministry to the point that we sometimes forget or neglect the pastoral part. There are so many needs that arise in our congregations that we become needs-based ministries. In other words, as we see a need arise in the congregation, we seek to supply ministries to meet that need. Our bulletins, websites and Facebook pages carry a plethora of programs that start on Sunday morning and end on Saturday night. As we seek to be all things to all people—even the copier machine says—give me a break. Church doors pre-pandemic were open 7 days a week and when they were closed during the lockdown, we were still on call 24/7 because we are trying our best to minster to hurting people during tough trying times.

Even casting the vision of financial stability for your home and family requires dirty work. You must establish financial goals and a budget but sometimes it's hard to stick to them because of lack of discipline around the dirty work. You must control spending; but people often overspend simply because they don't track their expenses. There are free apps that will help track daily expenses if you are unable or unwilling to do it manually. The dirty work of budgeting includes building up savings, savings for the future and for emergencies. For example, when the coronavirus pandemic hit America, most families were not prepared because they had **no savings for emergencies**. The same applied to small businesses especially businesses lead by people of color. **Because of wealth disparity and lack of access to capital among Black people 58% of Black-owned businesses were at risk of financial distress before the pandemic.** Due to the coronavirus shut down the number of working African American business owners in the US plummeted more than 40 percent. In an effort to save the economy, the government stepped in and extended unemployment payments, issued stimulus checks, and funded paycheck protection loans. Some Americans were receiving more money on unemployment than they were when they were working and still didn't budget. As a result, Americans not only got sick, but some got lazy. America, for the first time, has a labor shortage. When businesses reopened there were more jobs than people willing to work. Even now almost every business I see has a for hire sign out front. This labor problem in the US parallels what's happening in ministry. The harvest is plentiful, but the laborers are few.

With our will to work challenged, this is where the Vision Chaser has to step up and become the custodians and caretakers of the faith that was once delivered to the saints. Somebody has to do the dirty work by staying Vision focused and keeping everybody's eyes on the prize. Somebody has to be responsible for calling family meetings to review the budget and thank God for supplying all your needs according to His riches in glory.

Somebody has to discipline the family and say as for me and my house we shall serve the Lord. Somebody has to say No, that's not in the budget. We can't go out to eat, we need to go grocery shopping. Somebody has to remind everyone what the goals are for the family. The goal is to stop renting and owning. The goal is for retirement, vacation, college fund for children, investments, and the accumulation of wealth. But it starts with knowing that **the best way to live within your means is to live below your means.**

As Vision Chasers, we must always be prepared for emergencies. Since the pandemic everyone has been saying that they will be glad when things return back to normal. Unfortunately, things will never return back to the normal we once knew. But I can promise you that Jesus is coming back. He's coming back for a Church without spot or wrinkle. The church that was birthed on Calvary, baptized in the tomb, and came awake on Pentecost Morning. He has called Visionaries and left us in charge to get the people ready for His return. So, the house has to be cleaned. We must get rid of all the snakes and train some Ambassadors and Future Torch Bearers who can be effective in a Post Pandemic world.

Vision Chasers are called to be custodians of their own households but also the house of God. You are charged with cleaning it up and getting things right because a wedding is being planned. A marriage is about to take place. Our Savior is getting ready to make His return. I don't know what day. I don't know what hour, but I know we've got to be ready when He comes. We have to have our spiritual house clean when He comes. We can't clean it once and call it done. We have to keep on cleaning because dust will settle and accumulate. And if we are not ready, judgement will come and there will be no government bailout.

Paul charged Timothy with the duty of keeping the House of God clean. He left him with dirty work. He left him with the responsibility of being the Visionary, the Ambassador, and the Torch Bearer to carry on the work that had been started. They have done a marvelous ministry work in the city of Ephesus. In the two years that Paul preached in Ephesus, God moved in a mighty way because he did the dirty work. Many souls were saved. Warlocks and witches through away their documents, recanted and got saved. But Paul learned something that all Vision Chasers need to know; whenever God is using you to do major work, you must be ready for major opposition. Given our current crisis know that you are not assigned to preach and teach nursery rhymes. You are called and anointed to call out principalities and powers.

Paul tells Timothy that it's time for him to leave. But he couldn't leave the business of God without someone to carry the torch. Vision Chasers, this is a great work but to be successful you cannot do it alone. You are going to have to stand with the help of other Ambassadors, Visionaries and Torch Bearers as a team and do the dirty work. In the midst of this pandemic, the team will have to say: "why halt ye between two opinions. The team will be the ones crying over the burdens of God's people while feeling the weight of the pandemic. The team will stand up before God's people and tell them they better get their house in order. The team has to be united and stand on principal and refuse to bow down to idols and proclaim—BUT GOD! The team when everyone is full of doubt— when it seems like there is no way out to say He's Able and is there anything too hard for God. The team consist of those who have been called out and set apart to humble themselves. **James 4:6** states: "God opposes the proud; but gives grace to the humble. Vision Chasers have to humble themselves to do the dirty work.

Regardless of your official title, you are a servant of the most-high God. Your job as a servant is to keep the house clean, because a normal environment is not coming back but Jesus is coming back one day and when He does you want to hear him say—well done. If God has called you, that means He saw something in you. He knows that if you were to use what He sees in you—you can turn some lives around. He knows you can operate your business on Christian principals and lead your household by putting Him first. God has not blessed you, poured into you, and equipped you just so you can look sharp and pretty. He did it, so you could chase after Him and His will. He has done what he has done so you could be a custodian and a caretaker in a house, Church, city, county, state, and nation that needs to get right and get cleaned up. You are charged with doing the dirty work.

You might be wondering why God has so much confidence in you? He has confidence in you because He knows the fire that's inside of you and the torch that you carry for Him. He knows that you are filled with His power and when you speak, His power shall be revealed. Vision Chaser, God has confidence in you because He knows you will be true to His Vision and true to the Faith. God has confidence in you because He knows that your Theology is sound. God knows that you have a Theology of Providence verses a Theology of Prosperity. God has confidence in you because He know that you have a Theology of Glorification verses a Theology of Gratification. He knows that you would rather do good than feel good. So, beware of the spirit of self-gratification. Because it will creep into your ministry and business and have you putting profit over people. God has confidence in you because He knows you will have a theology of Theism rather than a theology of Me-ism. Me-ism means it's all about me. Theism means that it is all about God. God knows that you will have the ability to bring people together because of your theology. You will be able to do evangelism and community outreach—the dirty work of ministry. Theism says there is a God who sits high and looks low. I am a sheep in His pasture. He is the Great I Am. I live because He is. He speaks, and men live. He speaks, and men die. He is the creator of all. He has confidence in you because He knows your theology is real.

In order to be a Vision Chaser, you must become a decision maker that others can follow. Inability to make decisions is one of the principal reasons Vision Chasers fail. Every decision comes with risk. But decide anyway. The decisions you make will define your leadership and success. Don't shy away from them. Know your own weaknesses and surround yourself with Godly counsel and advisors to assist you in those areas. This alone with allow you to make sure you are making business decisions and not emotional decisions.

CEOs, Presidents, Senior Management, Supervisors, Senior Pastors, Bishops-the buck stops with you. You are the final decision makers. Granted, none of us are perfect and sometimes the decisions made are wrong; nonetheless, know that ultimately making a decision is always better than "no decision". Being a decision maker is dirty work because you are the one that has to make the tough calls. Even if everyone doesn't agree-and often times they wont—if the decision is made properly, it builds confidence and trust amongst the leadership team of Visionaries, Ambassadors, and Future Torch Bearers.

Vision Chasers are decision makers who live by example. Paul recognized that he had taught Timothy by example. Most people talk love, but don't show it. They are quick to talk forgiveness but won't put it into practice. Folks are quick to throw shade but never actually take a position on anything themselves. God has called you to show the standard even when you fall short of keeping the standard. He has called you to live by example. You've got to let your community know that God is Holy. God is just. Our God is righteous. Our God is omnipotent and a present help in times of trouble. Paul knew he could trust Timothy because he had exposed him to the living spirit of God.

Vision Chasers you have to know the Word to do the dirty work. God put Spirit and Word together. Jesus is the Word. In the beginning was the Word...they that worship Him must worship Him in Spirit and in Truth. It amazing how people want to be in the Spirit, but don't want to be in the Word. If you don't have the Word what does the Holy Spirit have to work with. He can't work with your opinion. He can't work with what you think, or feel is right. It's the Word that will help you in times of trouble. It's the Word that will hold you up when everything comes against you. It's the Word that will help you stand your ground in a spiritual fight. It's the Word that will teach you that no weapon formed against you will prosper. It's the Word that will teach you that the Lord is your light and your salvation. It's the Word that will confirm that in times of trouble, He will hide you. It's the Word that will tell you—ye thou He slay me—yet will I trust Him. It's the Word that says, All the days of my appointed time I'm going to wait until my change comes.

There are a whole lot of people out there who are leading

ministries, operating businesses, and serving as Head of Households that need to be lifted up themselves. The word says, "Some have wandered away and turned to meaningless talk." But talk doesn't get things done. Because of the pandemic many churches and businesses have closed or have simply become ineffective. As a Vision Chaser God is looking for you to shine during these dark times to lead His people back to Him. Remember you can take a rest, but you cannot quit.

God has confidence in you because He knows that you will recognize Him as the only celebrity in the Church and that you will continue to make business decisions using your Christian belief system. Out of all the people God could have called to run with His Vision, He chose you. He is trusting you to do the dirty work, because He has already done the dirty work on you. What can wash away your sins, nothing but the blood of Jesus. Vision Chasing is dirty work, and you have been called, anointed, and appointed to do it.

CHASE YOUR VISION-NOT SOMEONE ELSES'

If you are going to do the work of ministry, lead your household, or start a business as a Vision Chaser, make sure it's the work and vision that God has assigned to you. Don't try to be somebody else. Don't try to keep up with the Joneses. Your family budget is not the same as theirs. Don't try to preach and teach like somebody else. **Be you.** Don't start a business that is identical to the one across the street. Don't spend tireless hours trying to duplicate somebody else's' business plan. Your vision should show your uniqueness. Because can't nobody be you better than you can.

In **Acts 19:11-16** you will find words similar to these: "God did extraordinary miracles through Paul. So that when the handkerchiefs or aprons that had touched his skin—were brought to the sick, their diseases left them, and the evil spirits came out of them—Then some itinerant Jewish exorcists tried to use the name of the Lord Jesus over those who had evil spirits, saying, I adjure you by the Jesus whom Paul proclaims." Seven sons of a Jewish high priest named Sceva were doing this. But the evil spirit said to them in reply, "Jesus I know, and Paul I know; but who are you?" Then the man with the evil spirit leaped on them, mastered them all, and so overpowered them that they fled out of the house naked and wounded.". The point is that God has a work for you as a Vision Chaser. It is not necessary for you to attempt to be like anyone else. You don't need to preach like the person you see on T.V. You don't have to sing like the person getting thousands of views on YouTube. When you attempt to be someone else or perform like someone else, you are not effective. The only thing that you have accomplished is that you have taken extraordinary steps to poison your purpose and destroy your destiny.

Nothing can destroy your Vision's Destiny like jealousy and envy of another Vision Chaser. When we fail to find security and satisfaction in the work of our own hands, we manipulate our passions to imitate others. God has blessed you with the gifts necessary to not only chase the vision, but to capture and obtain it. So, instead of looking to others to copy or mimic, look into the mirror, and see the gifts that God has given you. You have tailor made talent, one-of-a-kind skills, dreams that can't be duplicated and a uniqueness that no one else can rob. So, it becomes necessary for you to know your gifts and celebrate them by using them daily to further the chase. Your gift is not something you had to buy; you were born with it. Others may not have appreciated or affirmed your gifts, but you need to celebrate them.

In this scripture, we see seven (7) sons (brothers) who fail to recognize the beauty of their own gifts. The Bible says they were Itinerant Exorcists—they worked in the business of healing. I am sure that in times past they had successfully healed the sick and delivered the possessed. However, one day they got word about the ministry of Paul. When they heard of Paul's success, they begin to lose confidence in their own gift. They became driven to become something that was not their divine purpose.

Scripture tells us that, all through the land, evil spirits were being passed out of people through the ministry of Paul. People were being healed and minds were being restored and regulated. There was a power in Paul that had no parallel in the eyes of the religious folk of that day. So, a fear and a jealousy begin to grow in the sons of Sceva. Because they, like so many of us, become insecure whenever we see someone else's success overshadowing our progress or stagnation. Sometimes the copy catting is done out of innocence-I've seen it done so I must do it that way or I see this is what works so why reinvent the wheel because God doesn't do carbon copies when it comes to the things of God. These seven (7) sons of Sceva are insecure and resentful of Paul or maybe they are just opportunistic. Nevertheless, they decide to gain success by imitating his gifts and power. When these seven (7) sons attempted to imitate Paul's actions, the evil spirit recognized that they had no power, no authority or anointing. They did not have a connection with the Holy Spirit. Evil knows what the anointing of the Holy Spirit looks like. Evil knows the difference between our authenticity and our deception. **Even evil can discern**! Evil can sift out the real, the fake and the phony. The point is that if you want God to do extraordinary things through you then you must be appointed and directly empowered by Him. This makes you fruitful and not ineffective, authentic, and not a counterfeit, successful and not frustrated. **That's why even today, you see so many people in ministries attempting to lay hands on people, falsely speaking into peoples' lives.... not because they have the power or the anointing to do so, but because they are seeking fame, fortune, and power over people.**

These seven (7) sons were so obsessed with the idea of Paul's fame and power that they tried to birth a miracle out of envy for selfish gain. The man with the evil spirit recognized the fraudulent gesture by these men and raised an important question. Jesus, I know. Paul, I know, but who are you? I know what Jesus stands for and the power that He possesses. I know the anointing of Paul and what he believes in. I can hear the spirit saying, "Jesus I know, that's God's son, Lilly of the Valley, Bright and Morning Star, the Greatest out pour of God's love—ever known." Paul, I know, that's God's servant and the Ambassador of Grace and the Torch Bearer of the Apostles. Love I know! Grace, I know, and I must yield to them! But to ego and envy and evil spirits just like me, I will not bow down.

You can't be in ministry or lead your home or business mimicking what you have seen others do. You have to be the best you. **Embrace that you are supposed to be different.** It's the reason you've been chosen. Your Vision should stand out from the crowd not blend in! As a Vision Chaser you can't allow yourself to become bound by jealously, greed and thirst for power. Granted sometimes copy catting is done out of innocence-I feel a call but this is the only way I've seen it done so I must do it that way or I see this is working, so why reinvent the wheel. But God doesn't do carbon copies when it comes to the things of God. You have been called to lead souls to Christ not to perform for Satan. Before you can do battle with the demons of others you will need to deal with your own. **Because when you stand before God on Judgement Day, He is not going to ask you about their demons He is going to ask why you didn't address yours.** These sons of Sceva think they are confronting evil when in fact they are actually exposing the evil, the sin that lives within themselves. Before you can Chase the Vision, you will have to wrestle and defeat the weak points of your character.

The scripture does not tell us exactly what the man was dealing with that the sons of Sceva were trying to deliver. What we do know is they called him an evil spirit. They labeled him evil. When they were the ones with envy and jealousy living inside of them. The last verse about the Sons of Sceva says, "The evil spirit so overpowered the sons of Sceva that they ran out of the house, naked and wounded." **We cannot allow ourselves to get so spiritually weak that evil spirits around us will cause us to run out of the house of God, naked and wounded.** When the devil wins a battle, it is time to look internally and face some issues and not massage your ego. It is time to be vulnerable enough, humble enough, exposed enough to change. If you forget about God and try to do things under your own strength, I can almost assure you that the enemy will leave you naked, wounded, and exposed.

It's time to come clean and drop the façade and say God I need you. I know I've been trying to make it on my own. I have even tried to imitate the gifts of others, because I had lost confidence in the ability you had given me. As a result, I lost my way and couldn't hear your voice. But here I am God, wounded and crying out. Please give me your grace and your mercy. Forgive me, for even thinking I could do anything without your guidance. Because now I see just how much your Word really applies to me. Because I am one of your people. You said, if my people would humble themselves and pray, seek your face, turn from their wicked ways. Then and only then can your healing power of grace and love begin to operate. Even the evil spirit said, "Jesus (love) I know. Paul (grace) I know. But ego and envy possess no power. Grace and Love have transformation power. Grace redeems and love pardons. But jealousy and envy will hold us captive.

We live in a world where money reigns supreme and governmental policies and media attempt to dehumanize. In this toxic environment, it's good to know that grace and love still trump hatred, envy, biases, prejudice, and jealousy. God is still in the saving business. So, stand up with your renewed strength and run this race with power. Chase and relentlessly pursue the Vision God has given you. Don't sell yourself short by trying to imitate the gift of others. Be an Ambassador of grace and love. Be the best you can be for God. He has equipped you for greatness.

GOD HAS A PLAN

THE DEVIL HAS A PLOT. GOD HAS A PLAN. Don't you just love it when a plan comes together. Because He has equipped you to chase the vision, He expects more from you. You are set apart for more. God has a plan for you to live holy in every area of your life. You might out sing, out dance, and outcry everybody in worship. But when you come down off your spiritual high, you are expected to live like you shouted.

Your Vision, Mission, Business Plan, Family Budget must include the plan God has for your life. In order to follow the plan--you must know the plan.

FIRST PLAN

You have to first know what Jesus did and why He did it. Jesus Christ is the only begotten Son of God the Father. Mary's baby. Jesus the son of a carpenter. Jesus who was educated in the public schools of Nazareth. Jesus the one who grew in favor with men. Jesus the one who was cheered as He rode down the Mount of Olives into Jerusalem. Yet before the week was over, those same people mocked, scorned, beat, and crucified Him. At one point the people were shouting Hosanna (save now) and Son of David (messiah-Savior). Even though they screamed and shouted Save-now Savior, Jesus was still persecuted. They were witnesses to him restoring sight to the blind. They saw evidence of him restoring lepers. They saw him feed the multitude with a schoolboys' lunch. They witnessed Him raise Lazarus from the dead. Jesus is the same one who healed the woman who was bent over for 18 years as well as the lady with the issue of blood for 12 years. They had listened to Him preach with authority and they believed that He was the one that would set them free. **(It's all a part of His plan.).**

Jesus had come to bring deliverance, but before the week was over, they were shouting crucify Him. The disciples had disappeared. They did not have the spiritual stamina to maintain their walk with Jesus. They had fizzled out. They lacked the emotional maturity or the fortitude to go all the way with Jesus. God has a plan for us through Jesus. It is the plan of salvation. The plan for our souls. God also has a plan for our lives. And a plan to use us for His purpose and glory.

SECOND PLAN

God's Plan is a plan of Salvation. You must follow the plan to chase the vision to continue to create an atmosphere where people can learn and accept the truth about the life, death, and resurrection of Jesus Christ.

Vision Chasers, your rest is over. The quarantine period of the pandemic is over. It is time to get back into the fight. It's war time. There is no quitting or second guessing your calling or anointing. In 2022, your anointing and your gifts will be needed more than ever before. You got this because Jesus Christ lives on the inside of you. You have been silent so long that people think you have quit. But there is no quitting on God. Can you imagine what you would be and where you would be if Jesus Christ had quit while He was in the garden. What if He had not elected to die? What if God, the creator of time, decided to go back and say, "you know what—I don't' think I will even create man. And if I don't create man, then I don't have to create woman. If I don't create them, then there will be no one for Satan to manipulate and temp into sin. If there is no one to temp, then there will be no sin. If there is no sin there will be no need for grace, mercy, favor, repentance, blessings, salvation, damnation, or hell. God said, I cannot go back on my word. God said, "I'm perfect. I cannot make a mistake. So, I have got to fulfil the plan.

Vision Chasers must make the same decision that Jesus did: not my will Lord, but your will be done. When you yield to God's will, you are submitting to God's plan. When Jesus submitted Himself to the Will of God, He did not have a choice about riding into Jerusalem. Imagine what your Christian walk would be if Jesus had not stuck to the plan. If He had not gone into Jerusalem, then there would be no Last Supper. If He doesn't have a Last Supper, He does not have the garden experience and the cup does pass Him by. If He doesn't go to the garden, then He would not have been betrayed by Judas. If He is not betrayed by Judas, then He does not get arrested. If He does not get arrested, He does not go before Pilate. If He does not go before Pilate, He won't be carried from Judgment Hall to Judgment Hall. If He is not dragged from one Judgment Hall to another one, then the crowd would never yell, crucify Him. If the crowd never yells crucify Him, then He would never have to carry the cross. If he never carries the cross, then He will never be crucified. If He is never crucified, then He will never bleed. If He doesn't bleed, then He doesn't die. If He doesn't die, then He can't be buried. If He is not buried, then there would have been no resurrection. If He had not risen, then He would not have rose with all power in His hand. If He did not rise with all power, then our salvation would be meaningless. If there is no resurrection, then He couldn't return to heaven. If He did not go back to Heaven, then you and I would not have an advocate sitting on the right hand of the Father. If He was not in Heaven, then the Holy Spirit could not have come to be our comforter. **It's all in the plan.**

THIRD PLAN

God's Plan is a plan of vision. Jeremiah 29:11 says, "For I know the plans I have for you, "declares the Lord, "plans to prosper you and not to harm you, plans to give you hope and a future. Hope of Heaven and a future without sin. There is victory in Chasing the Vision. Jeremiah tells the people that God has a promise for them. *After seventy years, God will bring you back just as He promised* **(Jer. 25:12). Chapter 29** is part of that promise. God says, "For surely I know the plans I have for you, plans for your welfare, not your harm, to give you a future and a hope." He finishes off this promise by saying, "Then when you call upon me and come and pray to me, I will hear you. When you search for me, you will find me. If you seek me with all your heart, I will let you find me," says the Lord, "and I will restore your fortunes and gather you from all the nations and all the places where I have driven you and bring you back." God always keeps His promises.

With Israel we see the faithfulness of God. In spite of their sin, He still considers them His people and has a plan for them. He promises to restore them as a nation. Likewise, He will restore you. After this pandemic is over, God is going to restore. So, run on Vision Chaser, it's all a part of God's plan. God has a plan that will impact us such as writing a book, starting a business, inventing a new App, or launching a new ministry. His plan began in a garden as a disobedient Adam and Eve and a treacherous serpent stand before God. God says to the serpent, ". . . and his heel will crush your head" **(Gen. 3:15).** *Victory will be mine. Evil will be overtaken.* God's plan continued when God tapped Abraham on the shoulder and said *I have plans to give you land and many descendants, to make you a blessing to the nations and all the peoples of the world* **(Gen. 13:14-16).** God has a plan. If you trust in Jesus Christ, God has already seen to your welfare in ministry, business, and family. You are the recipient of unsearchable riches, fortune, and an imperishable inheritance prepared for you in heaven. When everything lovely and gracious and pure in our world seems to fall victim to corruption and evil, God still has a plan for your future.

When the meek and the peacemakers and the pure in heart of God's kingdom get trampled into the dirt, when the weak are constantly sacrificed on the altars of power, God still has His plan. When it appears that this pandemic has no foreseeable ending, God still has a plan. It is a plan of love and grace, to save us and our vision. Despite the fact that we deserve nothing but God's condemnation of death, He has a plan of grace and mercy. Trust in the plan and the promises that God has given you in Christ. Go back and review the written Vision, your Mission Statement, your Business Plan. Chase after the Vision. Follow Jesus. Serve Him, obey Him, and trust Him in everything. Seek Him while He may be found with all your heart and be assured of this: absolutely nothing – **and I mean NOTHING** – can separate you from His love through Jesus Christ our Lord.

FOURTH PLAN

God's plan requires endurance and sacrifice. Sacrifice is a word that has been edited in the Christian vocabulary. Sacrifice has been deleted from the requirements of being a disciple. You got to have some sacrifice in your spirit. You got to learn to tell yourself no! You got to realize you can't have everything you want. Everything is not going to always be about you. You can't consume everything you want to consume. When you are chasing the vision—you've got to learn to let some things lay on the table and not put your hands on it. In order to make your business a success you have to make some sacrifices. Sticking to a budget requires making sacrifices. It's a part of proper financial management. Sometimes you have to cut cost, eliminate debt, and live within your means. Sacrifice helps us to become wise and accountable by using our resources responsibly.

You are a part of God's plan to bring Jesus to those who don't know him. You got to sacrifice in this plan. You got to surrender in this plan. Even the plan of salvation requires surrender.

You have got to make sacrifices for something bigger than yourself. Following God is not about getting your wish list filled. **Following God is not getting every prayer answered. Following God means he has positioned you in places where your sacrifice is required! It's all a part of the plan.**

THE PLAN IS BIGGER THAN YOU

Your business is bigger than you. Your Family Budget is bigger than you. Your ministry is bigger than you. When you are a part of something bigger, you have to have the strength to sacrifice.

It's good to look back and see just how far God has brought you and see just what this walk has cost you. It's good to look back and make a public confession that **it was good for me that I had been afflicted. (Psalm 119:71:75).** It took sacrifice for me to get here. For now, I truly know that life is a battle, whether you are prepared for it or not. **Hell is coming for you**—whether you want to participate or not. If you are chasing the Vision, the enemy is chasing you. You must have the faith to fight, outlast your troubles, to wait, be patient, to endure, to trust God, stand and keep chasing after His Will for your life. He has already supplied everything you need to be a success. If your greatest need had been information—God would have sent you an educator. If technology was your greatest need, he would have sent you a scientist. If your greatest need was money, He would have sent you an economist and a financial planner. If your greatest need had been to laugh and to have pleasure, He would have sent you an entertainer. But your greatest need was forgiveness and salvation so, He sent you a Savior. So, run on, run on, "Chase the Vision because you are chasing something bigger than you.

We are all a part of the plan. We should learn from Jesus before he went to the cross. Jesus stands in front of the pharisees, and they curse him and call him Beelzebub. He does not act out of anger and strike them dead. When Judas betrays him, He does not curse and damn Judas to hell. When He is on the cross and the thief and the crowd mock him, He doesn't come down and reveal His strength. He knew how to sacrifice. When Peter cuts the ear off of the soldier, He replaces it with his healing power instead of calling legions of angels to come to His defense. He knows everything He can do, He won't do, because He knows He is a part of something bigger than himself. Being a vision chaser means you are a part of something bigger than yourself.... **it's a part of God's plan.**

HAVEN'T SEEN YOUR BEST YET

GOOD, I SEE YOU ARE STILL BREATHING! If, you are still breathing, that means you haven't done your best work yet. So, get up and Chase the Vision. If tomorrow could talk it would tell you that God never starts anything that He does not have the power to complete. **Your best is yet to come because your vision quest is not finished. The resurrection reminds us that** God has the last word in our story. Your journey as a Visionary, Ambassador or Torchbearer is not yet complete. You are going to still have evil haters coming after you. As you rise many people will disapprove. **Rise anyway.** Because God has the last word. No weapon formed against you is going to prosper.

Your enemies do not have the last word. Your competitors do not have the last word. Injustice does not have the last word. But God shall supply all of your needs according to His riches in glory. All things will work out for your good. You may still be feeling tired and discouraged and think you can't go on. Remember God has the last word. Even though you may faint and be weary, young men may fall, but they that wait on the Lord—shall renew their strength. They shall mount up with wings like eagles, run and not get weary, walk, and not faint.

If God woke you up this morning, then you have not finished yet. You have not done your best work yet. So much has happened since the beginning of this pandemic and all of this post pandemic instability, but you are still standing because you are God's chosen

Vision Chaser. Vision Chasing takes time. Building a strong ministry with vibrant witness takes time. Reaching a new level in Jesus Christ takes **(the right mentor)** and time. Enduring hardship as a good soldier of Christ takes time. Developing that Business and restoring your community will take time. But do it. Get busy and do it. Don't just build a pile of money that's going to be worthless when you die. **Build a legacy. Leave an inheritance. It's time to Build up the kingdom of God here on earth.** Strengthen your faith and build honor to God

Every morning you have two choices: Keep sleeping with your dreams and visions or wake up and chase them. As the Covid-19 pandemic continues to shake the global economy, disrupts our old way of life and how business is done, and in person worship is held and how family develop thrives—we must look beyond the dark horizon and chase after the future. We must pivot toward success. We must revise and implement our strategic plans to meet new goals. We have to adjust to telecommuting, telemedicine and doctor visits, online shopping, online worship, digital media, broken global supply chains, millions of people out of work or refusing to work. The ultimate question for the Vision Chaser, is what's next? What is the long-term vision for your ministry, your business and your family. What updates should be made to your current written Vision, Business Plan and Family Budget? Where do you envision your ministry, your business and your family when the crisis of this pandemic is over?

We must envision what Christian worship and study will look like not just tomorrow but 5 to 10 years from now and work toward it. In your Christian business what will your customers, markets and operating environment look like 5 years from now.

How will they access your goods and services? What will be the method of payment for future goods and services? How will you keep Christ at the center of it all? How will you support building up the Kingdom of God in 2022 and beyond?

FAMILY BUDGET

What will be the long-term goals and objectives of the family budget? What strategy will you implement to ensure your success? What benchmarks and milestones will you utilize to help keep your eyes on the prize? It's time to review and study your monthly expenses to make sure your budget includes tithing, housing, utilities, food, credit card debt, car payments, life and burial insurance or a Pre-arranged Funeral Plan with a local funeral home. It should include gas, savings, and leisure expenses. Your emergency savings goal should increase to ensure that you amass enough money to cover three-to-six months of essential expenses. What investments should be given priority? Consult a financial planner if necessary. It's always great to check in and get somebody else's perspective on things to ensure that your legacy is secure. He who fails to plan, plans to fail. God is expecting you to use the time He has blessed you with to lead sinners into the faith of who He is. God is expecting you to get involved in **Christian Community Development and meet the needs of His people**. Throughout His Word our Lord is telling us kindly and encouragingly that, as long as we have our minds and can think, our vision mission is not over. We still have some work to do. If you are the head of an organization, business, or ministry you should be finding time to train other Visionaries, Ambassadors and future Torchbearers so that the legacy of your Vision continues long after you have gone.

VISION FOR MINISTRY FOR CHURCH, FAMILY & BUSINESS

Who have you designated as the future Torch Bearer for the Ministry or the Church? Who are the Ambassadors that will continue to keep the Vision moving forward long after you are done? Again, what leadership training are your providing? Who other than you is the visionary of your company or organization? Who is mentoring him or her to carry the Torch when you step down? How are you investing in key leadership to be Ambassadors, future Torch Bearers and Visionaries?

Who will be the next patriarch of the family? How are you training your children to not just have vision for themselves but for their current and future families? When they are no longer under your protection, have you given them a blueprint for spiritual and financial success? Have you imbedded the love of God in them that will sustain them for life and eternity? If you haven't and you're still breathing that means God is not done with you yet. You still have time. Don't live the day but learn to live every moment of the day. You must move your family forward during these trying times. Your Business Plan and your Household Budget are like road maps. You can't understand where you're heading if you don't have a map.

Leave a Legacy and an Inheritance. You can do this! You are a child of God. God will give you the anointing and the ability to go through the tough and rough spots without you falling apart. He will give you the ability to continue to go through these difficult moments without flipping out—to deal with haters and hell-raisers without going postal. As a Vision Chaser He will give you the strength to confront your critics, live through ridicule, survive the negativity and to battle with backstabbers. When you think about some of the hell you've been through and have overcome, you realize that you **were built to overcome**. Those scars you have aren't signs that you are finished. They're a sign that you've been healed. They're a sign that you are ready to move forward. The scars don't disqualify you; the scars are what prepared you for this very moment in time.

As long as you remember to wait on God and rest in Him, He will give you the ability to get to the boiling point and not boil over. To get to the edge of the cliff without jumping off. To get close to the fire and not be burned. To get lowered into the lion's den and not be eaten alive. To have you stand in front of the red sea and see it part in your favor. You are **going to keep your joy, your peace, your sanity, and your security** because He is going to sustain you through it all. So, even though you might be tested by fire, you shall emerge as pure gold.

Every day of your journey, God is maturing you and your vision is getting clearer. Perhaps for the first time, you see who is really for you and who is really against you. You see who is pushing you forward and who is holding you back. You have gotten to the point in your growth walk with God where you don't need external validation. You don't need other people to tell you it's alright before you can move. You know, and you've learned how to cast a Vision and Chase it. Maturity empowers you to embrace what God has prepared for you. God has matured you—so when you get to your next level—you will know how to handle it. He is going to enlarge your territory and expand your borders and enlarge your coast. You will be strong enough, wise enough, committed enough to manage the Vision quest that God has given you. As I stated in an earlier chapter, if you want to handle what God has for you, you've got to grow up! Maturity is your mandate. Not your happiness, comfort, or pleasure—but maturity.

No matter what has been said or done in your past, your best is still yet to come. God said even if you have broken all ten (10) commandments—He can still use you. You haven't done your best work yet. **Life is too short to have pity parties about yesterday.** It's time to get busy living and chasing after the vision God has promised. **THE PANDEMIC DOES NOT REQUIRE LESS OF US. IT REQUIRES MORE.**

You no longer have to do things or buy things to cover up what's inside of you. Your life is no longer about what you drive, but it is about what is driving you. Life is no longer about where you live, rather it is about what or who is living on the inside of you. You have been or can be delivered from all of your insecurities. You will chase the vision God has given you and not the vision he has given someone else. You will no longer compare yourself and compete with other people because deliverance has come.

Cornell West stated in an interview about America, "we are experiencing a spiritual eclipse of morality, deceit, integrity, honor and honesty." We are living in a nation of darkness-characterized by military madness, greed, and bold racism. All of this is going on in the darkness of America's spiritual eclipse. Additionally, we are now experiencing financial hardship in the middle of a pandemic.

If ever there was a time for America to have vision, it is now. We have been exposed to false theology. We have had to endure quarantine, the wearing of masks, gloves, social distancing, vaccines, and a virus that keeps mutating to a new strain. But glory to God we are all still standing. Matter of fact, when you God woke you up this morning, your enemies said, **"Oh no, here he/she comes again covered in favor and being followed by grace and mercy."** So, don't count yourself out. You can't lose. Failure is not an option.

It was February 3, 2007, in Johannesburg, South Africa. Laila Ali, the then 29-year-old daughter of boxing great Muhammad Ali, headlined as she defended her WBC and WIBA world titles against Gwendolyn O'Neil of Guyana. When Laila Ali came out for the fight the crowd was chanting against her. **They wanted her to fail.** They were cheering for her to lose because of who her father was. Her manager had a conversation with her while she was in her fight corner waiting for the bell to ring. He told Laila they want you to lose, because of who your father is. But I want you to win for the same reason, because of who your Father is. Laila, which means "goat" is an acronym for the **"Greatest of All Times"**. Her Father Muhammad Ali was called the "Greatest of All Times" in boxing. While standing in her fight corner, Laila was reminded of who she was. She got that inside her spirit and took that into the ring with her against Gwendolyn O'Neil. It took only 56 seconds and two stiff straight rights from Ali before the referee counted O'Neil out and the fight was over. When interviewed later, Laila said, I apologize to the fans for the brevity of the fight. But she declared in Ali fashion—"I forgot how good I was."

The devil wants you to lose, because of who your Heavenly

Father is. But you can't lose. **You have to win because of who your Father is.** Your Heavenly Father is the Greatest of All Times. He is Alpha and Omega. The Beginning and the End. You are fighting a good fight, and in the end-you shall win. Paul tells us, "I fought a good fight. I finished the race. I have kept the faith. **These three (3) phrases comprise an announcement of celebration and not a statement of sorrow.** Paul is telling us that he has lived life well. He has Chased the Vision with everything within him. He has no regrets because he has accomplished his purpose. He is confessing that he did his best while recognizing that he was not perfect. Nevertheless, he did not quit. He did not step back. He did not retreat. He lived out an unfailing commitment to God in Christ. He finished well and so will you. You will finish in faith because God built you to last. The visionary that has an authentic relationship with Jesus Christ and leads with God at the head of everything will emerge from this crisis with a ministry, a company, a family that is stronger and more resilient than they were before. You will be a **Vision Chaser Champion. You were built to last. You will finish strong. SO, NEVER, NEVER, NEVER STOP CHASING!**

Just like people in America and around the world are hoping that the pandemic will soon end, and things will return to normal again. Visionaries should always be looking forward to the next chapter. We should learn from our past, assess the present and declare the future. Denzel Washington is one of the greatest actors of our time. Once while being interviewed about one of his movies, he was asked what was his greatest work? Before Denzel could answer, the interviewer interjected; was it Training Day? You won an award for that movie. Denzel said, no that was a good one, first time I had played such a role—but that wasn't my best work. The interviewer said, was it "Fences" because you not only starred in that one, but you also produced and directed the movie. Denzel said no that was a great work, but it still wasn't my best work. He mentioned the "The Great Debaters, American Gangster, Inside Man, Antwone Fisher and others. The interviewer also mentioned "Malcolm X", and said, "you not only played Malcolm X, but you became Malcolm X." Again, Denzel responded in like fashion, no that was a good movie but that wasn't my greatest work. Finally, the interviewer asked, then what was your greatest work? Denzel responded, "**my next one.**" **Never give up, because you never know if the next try is going to be the one that works. Never Quit!**

www.ingramcontent.com/pod-product-compliance
Lightning Source LLC
Chambersburg PA
CBHW071450070526
44578CB00001B/293